THE AMERICAN CANCER SOCIETY

new HEALTHY EATING cookbook

Published by the American Cancer Society
250 Williams Street NW, Atlanta, GA 30303-1002
Copyright ©2016 American Cancer Society

Printed in the United States of America

Book design by Katie Jennings Campbell
Photography by Angie Mosier
Food styling by Jeanne Besser
Index by Deborah Patton

8 7 6 5   17 18 19 20

Library of Congress Cataloging-in-Publication Data
Names: Besser, Jeanne.
Title: The American Cancer Society new healthy eating cookbook / by Jeanne Besser.
Other titles: American Cancer Society's healthy eating cookbook | New healthy eating cookbook
Description: Fourth edition. | Atlanta, GA : American Cancer Society, [2016]
   | Series: Healthy for life | Revision of: American Cancer Society's
   healthy eating cookbook. 3rd. c2005.
Identifiers: LCCN 2016033353| ISBN 9781604432374 (paperback) | ISBN
   1604432373 (paperback) | ISBN 9781604432480 (kindle)
Subjects: LCSH: Cancer—Diet therapy—Recipes. | Cancer—Prevention. | BISAC:
   COOKING / Health & Healing / Cancer. | COOKING / Health & Healing /
   General.
Classification: LCC RC271.D52 A44 2016 | DDC 641.5/631--dc23 LC record
available at https://lccn.loc.gov/2016033353

For more information about cancer, contact your American Cancer Society at **800-227-2345** or **cancer.org**.

Quantity discounts on bulk purchases of this book are available.
For information, please send an e-mail to **trade.sales@cancer.org**.

For general inquiries about our books, send an e-mail to **acsbooks@cancer.org**.

American Cancer Society
Book Publishing
Senior Director, Journals and Book Publishing: Esmeralda Galán Buchanan
Managing Editor: Rebecca Teaff, MA
Senior Editor: Jill Russell
Book Publishing Manager: Vanika Jordan, MSPub
Editorial Assistant: Amy Rovere
Cancer Control Programs and Services
Senior Vice President: Chuck Westbrook
Managing Director, Content: Eleni Berger
Managing Director, Nutrition and Physical Activity: Colleen Doyle, MS, RD
Director, Cancer Information: Louise Chang, MD

THE AMERICAN CANCER SOCIETY

new HEALTHY
EATING
cookbook

FOURTH EDITION

JEANNE BESSER

CONTENTS

RECIPE LIST

MAIN COURSES

SOUPS, SALADS, SANDWICHES, AND SMALL MEALS

SIDE DISHES

BREAKFAST

SNACKS

DESSERTS

EXTRAS

Penne with Broccoli Rabe
and White Beans (page 80)

INTRODUCTION

IN A GIVEN DAY, we make more than two hundred decisions about what to eat and drink. *Two hundred.*

Think about that.

There is more evidence now than ever before that the choices we make about what we eat and how we live affect our risk for chronic diseases—from cancer to heart disease to diabetes to arthritis. Yet, it can be difficult for many people to adopt good eating and exercise habits in today's fast-paced, frenetic world. Even with willpower and resolve, we may have a lot of forces working against us: larger food portions, longer workdays and less time for exercise or cooking at home, and communities that aren't good for walking or biking.

Most people want to be healthier. They want to feel good and have more energy. And for most people, these things are possible, simply by making small, sustainable changes for the better.

Belief in what's possible drives *The American Cancer Society New Healthy Eating Cookbook, Fourth Edition.* This new edition represents the latest in scientific evidence about diet, exercise, and health. As the first book in our new *Healthy for Life* series, it is designed to make healthy eating—and living—more attainable, approachable, and workable for everyone.

As part of the American Cancer Society's mission to save lives, we want to share what we know to help people make positive changes. Each daily decision can be an opportunity to do something good for yourself.

So what will you find in this new edition?

To start, you'll find more than 120 new recipes, all taste-tested and reviewed by our medical staff and in keeping with our guidelines on nutrition. You'll find familiar flavors, as well as some dishes with international influences. Some recipes are easy to throw together with items you already have in your pantry, and others might introduce you to an ingredient you haven't tried before. All are simple, healthy, and above all, delicious.

You'll also find some nutritional basics and other information that can make healthy choices easier:

- The parts of a healthy diet

- The importance of portion control

- Tips to make cooking at home easier and more manageable

- Recipe indexes to make meal planning simpler

- How to understand food labels and interpret claims about the benefits of certain diets or foods

We also touch on ways to eat healthy on the run and give ideas for nutritious snacks to help you resist afternoon vending machine cravings. We offer guidance on making healthy choices when eating out—even how to make better fast food choices when you're on the road.

Finally, we also talk about simple ways to start incorporating more activity into your daily life, especially if you're not in the habit of exercising regularly. You don't have to be on a treadmill or in an aerobics class to be healthier. You just have to move.

Everyone can make one good choice. And if you can make one, you can make another, and another. So let's get started.

Seafood and
Shellfish Stew
(page 52)

HOW TO USE THIS BOOK

Make it your own

First, remember: cooking allows for a *lot* of adaptation.

Recipes aren't written in stone—they should be viewed as guides. If you don't like an ingredient, use less, leave it out, or choose a substitute. If there's something you love, add a bit more. Some recipes list optional ingredients—they will enhance the flavor and look of the dish, but are *not* essential! Take them or leave them—it's entirely up to you.

Read first!

Before you start cooking, always read through the entire recipe to get a sense of what's involved.

Make sure you have all the ingredients. It can be useful to line them up on your workspace in the order in which they're listed in the recipe. Move the ingredient aside or put it away after it's been used to be sure nothing is forgotten or added twice.

Note whether extra prep is involved or special equipment is needed. Is a nonstick or ovenproof pan recommended? Do you need a lid? Does the recipe call for a food processor or blender?

Keep it clean

A few simple strategies can help keep cleanup at bay:

Lining baking sheets with foil will keep cooked-on food from making the sheets hard to clean.

Reuse mixing bowls when possible, and always choose a bigger bowl than you think you will need; this will help prevent spills and keep you from having to switch to a larger one halfway through.

Keep a small container nearby for trash: this will prevent waste from piling up on your work surface.

If you use all of something, add it to the shopping list while it's fresh in your mind.

Choose carefully

For the best flavor, use kosher salt and freshly ground black pepper.

Use regular olive oil or canola oil for cooking and extra-virgin olive oil after cooking or in salads. Canola and olive oil can be heated to higher temperatures without burning, and cooking negates many of the qualities of extra-virgin olive oil. Cooking with these oils is also much more economical than extra-virgin olive oil.

Be picky when buying fresh produce. If you can, choose fruits and vegetables at the peak of their season.

In some recipes, you can use frozen fruits or vegetables. In many cases, they can be just as nutritious as fresh! Just be sure, when buying frozen fruit or vegetables, to steer clear of added sugar, butter, or sauces.

How to use the nutritional analysis

The nutrition information shown is for one serving, unless indicated otherwise. Ingredients that are optional or listed without a specific amount are not included. When a choice of ingredients is given, the first option was used in the analysis. If the recipe yield is given as a range (4 to 6 servings, for example), the analysis was done using the smaller number of servings. All data are rounded according to the U.S. Food and Drug Administration Rounding Rules.[1]

Enjoy yourself!

Cooking doesn't have to be a chore. Don't be afraid to try something new or be creative. Healthy eating is not only better for you, it's actually less work. The simpler the preparation, the easier it is for fresh and flavorful ingredients to shine through. So have fun!

Throughout the book, watch for these symbols, which signal the following types of information.

 A bit of advice to make the recipe easier, serving suggestions, and other useful information

 Substitutions for ingredients, variations in making a dish, or ways to make a meal more substantial

 A bit of trivia or information about an ingredient, a type of dish, or the nutritional content of a particular food

American Cancer Society Guidelines on Nutrition and Physical Activity[2]

Achieve and maintain a healthy weight throughout life.

- Be as lean as possible throughout life without being underweight.

- Avoid excessive weight gain at all ages. For those who are overweight or obese, losing even a small amount of weight has health benefits and is a good place to start.

- Get regular physical activity and limit intake of high-calorie foods and drinks as keys to help maintain a healthy weight.

Be physically active.

- Adults: Get at least 150 minutes of moderate intensity or 75 minutes of vigorous intensity activity each week (or a combination of these), preferably spread throughout the week.

- Children and teens: Get at least 1 hour of moderate or vigorous intensity activity each day, with vigorous activity on at least 3 days each week.

- Limit sedentary behavior such as sitting, lying down, watching TV, and other forms of screen-based entertainment.

- Doing some physical activity above usual activities, no matter what one's level of activity, can have many health benefits.

Eat a healthy diet, with an emphasis on plant foods.

- Choose foods and drinks in amounts that help you get to and maintain a healthy weight.

- Limit how much processed and red meat you eat.

- Eat at least 2½ cups of vegetables and fruits each day.

- Choose whole grains instead of refined grain products.

- If you drink alcohol, limit your intake.

- Drink no more than 1 drink per day for women or 2 per day for men.

WHAT IS A HEALTHY LIFE?

Ads for expensive exercise equipment and special diets can make healthy living look complicated. *Paleo, gluten-free, low-fat, low-carb, only eat these foods, don't eat these foods.*

The fact is no one superfood or food group is the magic bullet for good health (if only it were that easy!), and there is no secret to living a healthier life.

Here's the simple truth: making healthier choices doesn't have to be guesswork. Staying at a healthy weight, being active, and eating well are the best things we can do to positively affect our own health. Today, we know more than ever before about how to achieve these things.

▸ The diets shown to be healthiest share this in common:

  ◦ High intake of vegetables, fruits, whole grains, legumes, and nuts

  ◦ Moderate intake of low-fat and nonfat dairy products and alcohol

  ◦ Low intake of red and processed meats, sugar-sweetened food and beverages, and refined carbohydrates

▸ People who cook frequently at home eat better—less sugar, less fat, fewer refined carbohydrates, and less food in general—than people who cook less frequently or not at all.[3]

▸ Incorporating more movement into your everyday life—even just more time walking and less time spent sitting—is good for you in many ways.

▸ A healthy lifestyle reduces our risk of many chronic diseases, including cancer, heart disease, and diabetes.

WHAT DOES A HEALTHY DIET LOOK LIKE?

A healthy diet is made up of the following main components, all of which are essential to keep our bodies functioning at their best: protein, fats, carbohydrates, and vitamins and minerals.

Protein

Protein helps build and repair cells and keeps the immune system healthy. It can help you feel full longer and maintain a more balanced energy level. Protein is found in virtually every part of the body.

Some protein sources are better than others, of course. Limit red meat (beef, lamb, and pork) and processed meat (such as deli meats, hot dogs, and bacon); choosing leaner protein sources over red meat and processed meat may lower the risk of many chronic diseases.[4-9] (If you do eat red meat, eat smaller portions and leaner cuts. For example, if a recipe calls for ground beef, use the leanest percentage you can find, or try substituting ground turkey or chicken.)

Good Sources of Protein

‣ Poultry (especially white meat)

‣ Fish

‣ Eggs

‣ Beans

‣ Peas

‣ Lentils

‣ Nuts

‣ Nut butters

‣ Soy products

‣ Some whole grains

Recommendations vary for how much protein people should eat, depending on their age, activity level, and other factors. However, it's rare in the U.S. for people not to get enough protein. In fact, some experts think we eat too much protein.

In the United States, the recommended daily allowance of protein is 46 grams per day for women over 19 years of age, and 56 grams per day for men over 19 years of age.

But what does that look like?

It's one thing to know the recommendations, but what does that actually look like? Here are some healthy protein sources and how much they contain, for reference. The amounts may surprise you!

‣ 3 ounces chicken breast without skin = 28 grams protein

‣ 6 ounces Greek yogurt = 18 grams protein

‣ 3 ounces salmon = 22 grams protein

‣ ½ cup pinto beans = 11 grams protein

‣ ½ cup tofu = 10 grams protein

Animal sources and plant sources of protein are different: plant sources are missing some amino acids found in animal proteins. Thus, it's important for vegetarians to eat a variety of types of plant-based proteins.

Fats

Your body needs fat to function properly. Fat helps build new cells, provides energy, and helps with important bodily functions. There are different kinds, though, and the type of fat you eat—not just the amount—has an effect on overall health.

It's now believed that there are healthy fats and unhealthy fats, and the "good" fats are an important part of a nutritious diet.[10]

The "Good" Fats

Monounsaturated fats – found in canola, peanut, and olive oils; avocados; nuts such as almonds, hazelnuts, and pecans; and seeds (pumpkin and sesame seeds)

Polyunsaturated fats – found in corn, sunflower, flaxseed, and safflower oils; walnuts; and many types of seafood, including salmon, tuna, and mackerel, which contain omega-3 fatty acids

The "Bad" Fats

Saturated fats – found in animal foods, such as meat and dairy products, and in coconut, palm, and palm kernel oils. Also called solid fats, saturated fats are not believed to be as harmful as trans fats.

Trans fats – found primarily in processed foods that contain partially hydrogenated oils, they're added to foods to improve shelf life, flavor stability, and texture. Trans fats are found in red meats, butter, and milk in small, naturally occurring amounts, but those are not thought to have the same harmful effects as trans fats in processed foods.

There is still debate as to how much fat intake affects overall health. Some argue that diets high in fat also tend to be high in calories, leading to unnecessary weight gain, whereas others assert that a high-fat diet can be healthy, if the type of fat is the "right" kind.[11,12]

The bottom line is that many of the foods containing healthy fats—salmon, nuts, avocado, for example—are also good sources of other nutrients. For now, the best bet seems to be including healthy fats in your diet while still being mindful of overall caloric intake.

Carbohydrates

Carbohydrates provide quick sources of energy to fuel the body. Like fat, carbohydrates have gotten a bad reputation in recent years. However, they are important fuel for your body.

The amount of carbohydrates you eat is less important than the type you eat. Simple carbohydrates are sugars—white sugar, honey, brown sugar, etc.—and are digested very quickly, leading to rapid increases in blood sugar levels. Complex carbohydrates, on the other hand, are digested more slowly and help maintain more even blood sugar levels.

Healthier Carbohydrates

- ‣ Whole grains
- ‣ Beans
- ‣ Lentils
- ‣ Fruits
- ‣ Vegetables

Unhealthy Carbohydrates

- ‣ White bread
- ‣ Pastries, cakes, donuts
- ‣ Sodas and other sweetened beverages
- ‣ French fries
- ‣ Other highly processed or refined foods

Most of us will remember the low-fat diet craze of the 1980s and 1990s. When the advice to follow a low-fat diet became the law of the land, people began to eliminate all fat from their diets. Food companies rushed to create low-fat and fat-free products, but in place of fat, they added refined carbohydrates and sugar.

It's now believed that the increase in refined carbohydrates and sugars in the diet actually made our health worse, contributing to higher rates of obesity and diabetes. Research shows that instead of eliminating all fat, a better approach is to limit saturated fat and trans fats, but to replace them with healthy fats, especially polyunsaturated fats.[13-16]

The healthiest food sources of carbohydrates provide vitamins, minerals, other important nutrients, and fiber.

What Is Fiber?

Fiber is a type of carbohydrate the body can't digest. It's not broken down into sugar like other carbohydrates, and so passes through the body undigested. Most plentiful in whole grains—but also found in fruits, vegetables, nuts, seeds, and beans—fiber slows the breakdown of starch into glucose, helping to maintain steadier blood sugar levels. Fiber from whole grains may help lower cholesterol and the risk of obesity, heart disease, stroke, and type 2 diabetes.

Most people in the U.S. don't get nearly enough dietary fiber. According to one source, Americans eat on average fifteen grams of fiber per day. Compare that to the figures below.

Daily Recommended Fiber Intake for Adults

Men 50 or younger—38 grams

Men 51 or older—30 grams

Women 50 or younger—25 grams

Women 51 or older—21 grams

There are two types of fiber—soluble and insoluble—and both are needed for a healthy diet. Soluble fiber dissolves in water and can help lower blood glucose levels and blood cholesterol. Insoluble fiber, on the other hand, does not dissolve in water and aids in moving food through the digestive system, helping prevent constipation.

Sources of Soluble Fiber

- Oatmeal
- Nuts
- Beans
- Lentils
- Apples
- Blueberries

Sources of Insoluble Fiber

- Wheat and whole grains
- Brown rice
- Legumes
- Carrots
- Tomatoes
- Cucumbers

What About Cholesterol?

Cholesterol is a waxy substance found in all cells of the body. There are two types: LDL, the "bad" cholesterol, and HDL, the "good" cholesterol. High cholesterol raises the risk of health problems, including heart disease, heart attack, and stroke.

People with high cholesterol have long been told to avoid foods that contain a lot of cholesterol, such as egg yolks and shrimp. But research now shows there isn't a strong relationship between the amount of cholesterol in our bloodstream and how much cholesterol a person actually eats. [11,17-19]

Diet does play a role, but in a different way from once thought. The biggest dietary influence on blood cholesterol levels is actually the mix of fats and carbohydrates in your diet. Saturated fat and trans fats both raise levels of bad cholesterol, and trans fats also lower levels of good cholesterol.

For some people, high blood cholesterol is simply a case of genetics. And for a select minority, dietary cholesterol has a strong influence on overall blood cholesterol. But doctors are not yet certain why that is or how best to identify those people. Many doctors still advise people to be aware of their intake of foods high in cholesterol. But the role of these foods is still under debate.

Vitamins and Minerals

Vitamins and minerals help the body work as it should—helping cells and organs function, supporting growth and development, and strengthening the immune system. They are found in varying concentrations in many foods, and so the best way to get what you need each day is to eat a variety of healthy foods: fruits and vegetables, whole grains, low-fat dairy products, fish, and lean meats and poultry.

Some vitamins and minerals act as antioxidants, substances that can stop the damage caused by free radicals in the body. Antioxidants are widely promoted as helping prevent a range of ailments, but proof is relatively modest. Studies suggest that people who eat more vegetables and fruits, which are rich sources of antioxidants, may be at a lower risk for cancer and other diseases. However, these foods also contain many other compounds, so it's not possible to say for sure how much antioxidants contribute to this lower risk.

Good Sources of Antioxidants

▸ **Vitamin A:** milk, liver, butter, and eggs

▸ **Vitamin C:** most fruits and vegetables, especially oranges, cantaloupe, kiwi, strawberries, papaya, broccoli, Brussels sprouts, tomatoes, cauliflower, kale, and bell peppers

▸ **Vitamin E:** some nuts and seeds, such as almonds, sunflower seeds, hazelnuts, and pecans; leafy green vegetables; and soybean, sunflower, corn, and canola oils

▸ **Beta-carotene:** colorful fruits and vegetables and leafy green vegetables

▸ **Lutein:** leafy green vegetables

▸ **Lycopene:** pink and red fruits and vegetables

▸ **Selenium:** cereals, nuts, legumes, animal products, bread, and pasta

There is also growing evidence that eating more fruits and vegetables can help control weight, though it may depend on which ones you eat. One study indicated that produce with a lot of fiber and a low glycemic index could help a person get to and stay at a healthy weight.[20] For example, berries, citrus fruits, and soy seemed to be associated with lower weight gain over time, while starchy vegetables, such as peas, potatoes, and corn, were not. Your best bet? Eat a large variety of fruits and vegetables and include them at every meal and for snacks.

Calcium and Dairy

Calcium is the most abundant mineral in the body, and for most people in the U.S., most dietary calcium comes from dairy products. There is still debate, however, about whether dairy is the best source of calcium for most people and about its role in overall health. Dairy products can be high in saturated fat, and high dairy intake may increase the risk for some cancers. If you do consume dairy, choose lower-fat sources. Non-dairy sources of calcium include bok choy, soybeans, collard greens, kale, and canned salmon, sardines, and shrimp.

Sodium and Sugar

Two dietary elements that are increasingly seen as problematic are sodium and sugar, both of which are abundant in processed foods and in the typical American diet.

Sodium

Almost 90 percent of Americans age two and over consume too much sodium.[21,22] Ninety percent! Eating too much sodium is associated with an increased risk of stroke, heart disease, osteoporosis, stomach cancer, and kidney disease.

The government recommends limiting daily sodium intake to 2,300 milligrams (one teaspoon). However, the American Heart Association recommends a limit of 1,500 milligrams for the following at-risk individuals:

- People over the age of 50
- People who have elevated blood pressure
- People who have diabetes
- African Americans

More than 75 percent of the sodium we eat is in processed and prepared foods—and some of the sources may surprise you:

- Deli meats
- Canned soups and vegetables
- Condiments
- Breakfast cereals
- Frozen meals
- Bread and tortillas
- Dairy products, especially cheese

Sugar

Sugar, or more specifically *added sugar,* is another part of our diet that is getting an increasing amount of negative attention. Not all sugar is bad—natural sugars are found in foods that play an important role in a varied, healthy diet. But as far as our bodies are concerned, sugar is sugar.

The difference lies in the *types of foods* that contain the sugar. Fruit contains sugar but is also a good source of vitamins, minerals, and fiber. Added sugars, on the other hand, are usually found in foods that have no nutritional value, such as sweetened drinks, donuts, cookies, and cakes. Added sugars can lead to unhealthy weight gain, which increases your risk for cancer, diabetes, and heart disease.

How Much Sugar Is Too Much?

Advice on sugar consumption can be confusing. Guidelines vary, and depending on the source, the terminology jumps between grams, teaspoons, and percentage of calories. See the box below for guidance from several prominent organizations for sugar consumption. What do we do with these conflicting numbers?

To start, take a look at the facts. For Americans, the average intake of added sugar per day is **twenty-two teaspoons**, or **eighty-eight grams**, and half of this consumption comes from sodas and other sugary drinks.[23] So even in comparison to the most lenient guidelines, we consume twice as much sugar as is recommended.

Added sugars can also pop up in some surprising places:

- Some brands of store-bought spaghetti sauce have as much as twelve grams of sugar in a half cup!

- Store-bought barbecue sauce can contain up to fifteen grams of sugar in two tablespoons.

- A "snack-pack" pudding (designed with kids in mind) can contain between fifteen and twenty-one grams of sugar in one small cup.

Guidelines for Sugar Consumption

Federal Dietary Guidelines

- 10 percent or less of daily calories *OR* twelve teaspoons per day for an adult

World Health Organization

- 5 percent or less of daily calories *OR* six teaspoons per day

American Heart Association

- Women: Six teaspoons (twenty-four grams) per day

- Men: Nine teaspoons (thirty-six grams) per day

*Note: One teaspoon of granulated sugar=four grams

INGREDIENTS THAT SIGNAL ADDED SUGAR IN FOODS

Although nutritional labels may list added sugars on a separate line from naturally occurring sugars, there are other ways to spot added sugars in your food. If any of the terms below appear in the ingredient list, the food in question has added sugar.

Brown sugar	Fruit juice concentrate	Maltose	Cane crystals
Corn sweetener	Glucose	Malt syrup	Cane sugar
Corn syrup	High fructose corn syrup	Molasses	Crystalline fructose
Dextrose	Invert sugar	Raw sugar	Evaporated cane juice
Fructose	Lactose	Sucrose	Corn syrup solids
		Sugar syrup	

Sodas and Obesity

Two of three adults and one of three children in the United States are overweight or obese.[24,25] Our increased consumption of sugar—particularly in sodas and other sugary beverages—is a major contributing factor to this trend in weight gain. Half the people in the U.S. consume at least one sugary drink per day. Sugar intake has also been linked to an increased risk of such chronic diseases as diabetes and heart disease, in addition to other health risks associated with obesity.[26-30] Studies in children and adults have shown that reducing consumption of sugary drinks helps with weight control.[31,32]

Since the 1950s, when standard soda bottles were 6.5 ounces, drink sizes have steadily increased. Today, a 20-ounce soda bottle is considered the norm by many; a 20-ounce soda contains 15 to 18 teaspoons of sugar and more than 240 calories.[33-36]

A large soda might contain as many as 700 calories, but drinking those calories does not feel the same to our bodies as eating them. Therefore, the calories that come from sugary drinks are truly "empty calories."[33,37,38]

Portion Control and a Healthy Diet

In addition to thinking about *what* you eat, it's also important to think about *how much* you're eating. Portion control is an essential component of a healthy diet, but it can be easier in principle than in practice.

▸ A **serving** is a specific amount of food or drink, such as ½ cup of broccoli, which is established by the United States Department of Agriculture (USDA). It is the basis for the information on the Nutrition Facts Panel on packaged foods.

▸ A **portion**, however, is the amount of food that you actually eat at one time—which can be bigger or smaller than the recommended serving size.

For many of us, the first step to being more mindful of portion size is simply to remind ourselves of standard serving sizes. Look at the chart below. How do these serving sizes compare to what you might receive at a restaurant or serve yourself at home?

FOOD	VISUAL CUE	
1 cup broccoli	Baseball	
Potato	Computer mouse	
Medium apple or orange	Tennis ball	
½ cup chopped or cooked fruit	Computer mouse	
½ cup brown rice	Computer mouse	
1 cup pasta or dry cereal	Fist (with fingers tucked in)	
2-3 ounces cooked meat, poultry, or fish	Deck of cards	
2 tablespoons peanut butter	Ping pong ball	
¼ cup dried fruit	Ping pong ball	

Controlling Portion Size at Home

▸ Don't eat from the bag, especially when you're watching television. It's easy to eat more than you realize when you're distracted.

▸ Don't estimate serving sizes—measure! Use a measuring cup to pour cereal and measuring spoons for cream or sugar when you add them to your morning coffee. Measure oils instead of pouring them.

▸ If you buy foods in bulk, measure and store individual servings separately.

▸ Replace larger plates with smaller ones, or try using small plates for entrées and large plates for salads.

▸ Portion out food in the kitchen instead of placing serving dishes at the table family-style so you are less tempted to have a second helping.

Read the Label!

For packaged foods, read the label! The food's label is a source of important information, including the serving size, calories, and ingredients. The labeled serving size can help you gauge how many calories you're taking in each day.

▸ How big is a serving?

▸ How many servings are in the package?

▸ How does the serving size relate to what you would typically eat or drink?

Typical portion sizes have grown drastically since the early 1970s and are often much bigger than the serving sizes listed on packaged foods and drinks. Many of us have lost sight of just how many calories we're taking in.

Look at the nutrition facts panel. How much sodium is in a serving? How much fiber or sugar? Read the ingredients list. Ingredients are listed in order of quantity, which can help you get an idea of what you're really buying. You can also look for "hidden" ingredients—added sugars, trans fats, items that aren't necessarily listed on the nutrition facts label.

Ways to Make Healthy Eating Easier

We've covered what to eat and how much, and now the next step—how to make it easier to make good choices.

Simplifying Home Cooking

Cooking frequently is associated with eating a healthier diet, regardless of whether you are trying to lose weight. When people cook most of their meals at home, they eat fewer carbohydrates, less sugar, and less fat than those who cook less or not at all.[3]

This isn't surprising. When you cook at home, you are more aware and more in control of what goes into your food and how it's prepared. By using as many fresh or minimally processed ingredients as you can, big improvements will be easier than they seem.

These simple strategies can make home cooking easier:

▸ If you don't cook regularly, start gradually. Begin by making dinner once or twice a week and work your way up.

▸ Schedule time each week to plan the week's meals. Some people do this on the weekend, some do it Monday morning once the kids are off to school—find a time that works with your schedule. If possible, keep recipes and coupons in a dedicated spot.

▸ Think about the week ahead of you, and take advantage of the recipe lists on pages 210–213. For a hectic weeknight, choose a dish that can be put together quickly or prepped before work. If you're making a dish that would freeze well, double the recipe and freeze half.

▸ Get the whole family involved! Let family members choose or vote on dishes. Kids can wash produce and, depending on their ages, do some chopping or measuring. The more involved children are with making the meal, the more likely they are to try new foods.

▸ Keep your kitchen organized. If ingredients and equipment are easier to find, it will shorten prep time.

▸ When you're making your grocery list, check to see what you have on hand so that you don't buy duplicates or miss any ingredients. A thorough list will help prevent impulse purchases and keep you from having to make a second grocery run later in the week!

▸ Make shopping easier by organizing the list according to the store's layout, or use prepared lists with foods you buy frequently so you only have to mark what you need or add new items.

▸ Keep healthy staples on hand so that you can put together a meal quickly.

PANTRY STAPLES FOR HEALTHY EATING

Use this list as a starting point and add or take away according to your likes and dislikes.

IN THE CUPBOARD

- Dried beans and lentils

- Canned no-salt-added beans, such as black beans, chickpeas, cannellini beans, pinto beans, kidney beans, black-eyed peas, and vegetarian refried beans

- Grains, such as brown rice (and instant brown rice), quinoa, wheat berries, bulgur, barley, and millet

- Seasoned or plain bread crumbs, panko

- Pastas, including orzo, soba, macaroni, and rice noodles, and whole wheat pastas, such as spaghetti, penne, bowtie, and couscous

- Whole wheat crackers, whole grain cereals, and popcorn

- Hot cereals, such as oatmeal (steel-cut, quick-cooking, and rolled)

- Canned tomatoes (diced or whole), salsa, pasta sauces (but watch for added sugar)

- No-sugar-added applesauce and canned fruits in 100 percent juice

- Dried fruits, such as raisins, dates, figs, apricots, prunes, and blueberries (preferably without added sugar)

- Reduced-sodium canned broths

- Canned tuna or salmon (packed in water)

- Peanut butter (preferably all-natural) and other nut butters

- Unsalted raw nuts, such as almonds, walnuts, and cashews

- Vinegars, such as balsamic, red wine, white wine, rice, apple cider, and sherry

- Oils, including olive oil, canola oil, dark sesame oil, and nonstick cooking spray

- Condiments, such as reduced-sodium soy sauce, mirin, chile-garlic sauce, and Worcestershire sauce

- Sun-dried tomatoes

IN THE REFRIGERATOR

- ‣ Fresh vegetables and fruits
- ‣ Nonfat Greek yogurt
- ‣ Reduced-fat or regular cheeses
- ‣ Corn or whole wheat tortillas
- ‣ Eggs
- ‣ Minced garlic

IN THE FREEZER

- ‣ Frozen vegetables, such as edamame, peas, spinach, broccoli, corn, and mixed vegetables
- ‣ Frozen fruits, such as berries and peaches
- ‣ Chicken breasts and ground turkey breast
- ‣ Fish, such as salmon, flounder, tilapia, and red snapper

Healthy Snacking Strategies

Whether you're fighting the afternoon munchies at the office or trying to help your kids nibble something besides Goldfish, snacks are part of life. With a little planning, you can have something handy to grab and go and still give your body the nutrients it needs, with fewer calories and less fat and sodium!

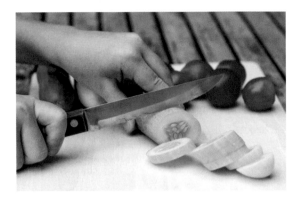

- Plan ahead. When you buy fresh fruits and vegetables, do some prep work right away. Wash whole fruits such as apples and pears and cut enough fresh fruit or veggies for a couple of days' snacking so they're ready to grab and eat.

- Put nutritious snacks where you can see them. Put cut fruits and vegetables at eye level in the refrigerator and place the fruit bowl in eyesight.

- Make a list of healthy snacks in the fridge and post it on the door, so you remember what you have on hand.

- If you're in your car a lot, keep a stash of healthy snacks that don't need to be refrigerated in your glovebox or bag.

- If you do have junk food on hand (this may be particularly likely if you have teenagers!), employ the stepladder rule. Put those foods where they're not easily accessible. If you have to get the stepladder to reach potato chips, you might be more likely to make a different choice.

- Take fresh fruit to work, but also keep nonperishable snacks on hand for days when you forget. Homemade or store-bought trail mix, unsalted nuts, dried fruit, whole grain dry cereals, and prepackaged fruit in 100 percent juice are all good possibilities.

SNACKS TO KEEP ON HAND

‣ Fresh vegetables cut into snack-sized portions, such as carrot and celery sticks, bell peppers, jicama, or zucchini cut into strips, broccoli or cauliflower florets, cherry or grape tomatoes, and snow peas. (If you're short on time, many supermarkets sell packaged, ready-to-eat vegetables, although you'll pay a premium for the convenience.)

‣ Fresh fruit, such as pears, apples, oranges, nectarines, peaches, kiwi, grapes, berries, melon, and bananas. (Again, many grocery stores sell precut melon and other fruits.)

‣ No-sugar-added applesauce or packaged fruit in 100 percent juice

‣ Small portions of dried fruit, without added sugar if possible

‣ Frozen grapes, cherries, blueberries, and raspberries for smoothies or for eating on their own

‣ Unsalted sunflower seeds, almonds, walnuts, and other nuts

‣ Whole grain, low-sugar breakfast cereals

‣ Air-popped popcorn

SNACKS WITH STAYING POWER

Snacks that include fiber, protein, and healthy fats can help you stay full longer, but watch portion sizes and be mindful of calories.

‣ Small portions of hummus with veggies or whole grain crackers

‣ Steel-cut oatmeal with fruit

‣ Whole wheat crackers or unsalted rice cakes with nut butter

‣ Nonfat Greek yogurt with berries

‣ Homemade trail mix with whole grain cereal, dried fruit, unsalted nuts, and a few dark chocolate chips, if you need a touch of sweetness

‣ A fruit and protein pairing (an apple or banana with peanut butter, apple or pear with cheese, ants on a log, low-fat cottage cheese and fruit, for example)

‣ Smoothies (with yogurt or even natural peanut butter added to make them more filling)

‣ Homemade mini pizzas, using whole wheat English muffins or tortillas

Eating Healthy When Eating Out

Eating out shouldn't feel like deprivation any more than eating healthy should!

- Decide where the calories count most. If you love dessert, order it and have an appetizer as your main course, or split dessert with your dining companion. If fries are your most sacred indulgence, watch your portion size and skip other high-calorie parts of the meal.

- Look at the restaurant's menu online before you head out, and decide in advance what you'll order. If you can't do that, be prepared to look for healthier menu choices.

- Salads can contain loads of unhealthy fats and calories thanks to heavy dressings or toppings such as cheese or croutons. Look for salads that contain a lot of veggies and include a healthy protein, like grilled chicken, beans, or chickpeas. Seeds or nuts can add healthy fats, but watch quantities. Ask for dressing on the side and dip your fork into the dressing and then into your salad rather than pouring it directly on top, or ask for oil and lemon juice or balsamic vinegar and lightly dress it yourself.

- Don't be afraid to ask how a dish is prepared or ask for healthier substitutes.

- Have the server remove the bread basket or bowl of chips from the table, and drink water or unsweetened tea instead of soda or other sweetened beverages.

- Practice portion control—have an appetizer as your main course or share an entrée with a friend and order a small side salad.

If you order a full-size entrée, ask for an extra plate so that you can divide the dish and have that portion wrapped up.

The Fast Food Challenge

It's fast, easy, it tastes good, and it's cheap. There are lots of reasons people cruise through fast food restaurants, and good nutrition is not usually one of them. But it is possible to make wiser choices and eat a *relatively* healthy meal.

- Order items without cheese or calorie-rich toppings like bacon, sauces, and mayonnaise. Add flavor and crunch with mustard, lettuce, tomato, and onion.

- If you're ordering chicken, stick with grilled options. Beware of buttered or mayo-slathered buns, too.

- Ignore combos, and skip anything with words like super-size, jumbo, giant, deluxe, or biggie-sized.

- Order a junior-sized sandwich or kid's meal. Many restaurants offer kid's meals with fruit instead of fries. If you can't resist fries, get the smallest size and add a side salad.

- If you can, park and walk inside. We could all benefit from walking whenever we can. It's better for you, and sometimes it's even faster!

Physical Activity and a Healthy Life

Getting regular physical activity is one of the most important things you can do to improve your overall health.

Physical activity can—

- Help you lose weight or stay at a healthy weight
- Reduce stress
- Alleviate depression and anxiety[39]
- Lower your lifetime risk for chronic diseases, such as heart disease, diabetes, stroke, and cancer

The American Cancer Society recommends that adults get *at least* 2½ hours of moderate-intensity aerobic activity or 1¼ hours of vigorous-intensity aerobic activity each week (or a combination of these), preferably spread throughout the week. This level of activity has been shown to have clear health benefits. More activity is likely to provide even more benefits.

Moderate-intensity activities will make you breathe as hard as you would during a brisk walk, but you should still be able to carry on a conversation.

- Walking quickly
- Dancing
- Biking (leisurely)
- Yoga
- Doubles' tennis
- Golfing
- Lawn and garden work
- Vigorous housework

Vigorous-intensity activities should make your heart beat faster and make you use large muscle groups, sweat, and breathe faster and deeper. You should still be capable of having a conversation, but your sentences will be shorter.

- Jogging or running
- Swimming
- Biking (fast)
- Aerobics
- Weight training
- Soccer
- Singles' tennis
- Cross-country skiing

It's not certain, but it's thought that getting activity even in bursts of ten minutes is as effective for overall health as longer stretches of exercise.

The Physical Activity Guidelines for Americans also recommend that adults do muscle-strengthening exercises—such as weight-lifting or using resistance bands—two or more days a week. Strength training has many health benefits, such as increasing lean body mass and decreasing fat mass.[40] It can also be an important part of maintaining vitality and function as we age, and can help older adults with basic activities like rising from a chair, climbing stairs, and walking.[41-48]

If you haven't been active in some time or have never exercised regularly, start with moderate activities and slowly increase the duration, frequency, and intensity. Don't try to run a half marathon if you haven't exercised in years! Be sure to check with your doctor first if you have concerns.

It can take some time for a new habit to stick. If you miss a day, don't give up—just get right back on track and keep moving forward.

Steps to Loving Exercise

Physical activity doesn't have to be a chore—when you pick an activity that suits your personality and needs, it's more likely you'll stick with it and get more benefit.

Do you like to be social, or would you prefer time to yourself?

- Social butterflies should try activities that connect them with other people, like walking with friends or joining a team or recreation association.

- If you need time to yourself, consider walking, running, swimming, or gardening.

Simple Safety Tips

- Warm up and stretch to reduce chance of injury.

- Drink plenty of water before, during, and after physical activity.

- Don't overdo it. There is no gain from pain.

- Always follow instructions and safety recommendations when using exercise equipment or machinery.

Do you need to get energized or wind down?

▸ For an energy boost, try aerobic activities that get the heart pumping.

▸ Reduce stress with yoga or tai chi.

Are you goal-oriented, or do you like to stay flexible?

▸ If you like a sense of accomplishment, try an activity where you can monitor your progress, like training for a run, or take up an activity with rising skill levels, like martial arts.

▸ For more flexibility, try walking or find an exercise video you can do at home.

Do you want to get away from it all or get involved?

▸ If you want escape, try outdoor activities like hiking, biking, or rollerblading.

▸ Get involved while you get active by building homes for the disadvantaged, taking part in charity walks and runs, helping an elderly neighbor with yard work, or tidying up a local school.

Easy Ways to Be More Active Without a Gym Membership

▸ Walk! It's free, and the only thing you need are some good walking shoes. And it burns calories: a 150-pound person walking briskly can burn 297 calories per hour. You can even turn it into a friendly competition. Wear a pedometer or activity tracker every day and see who among your family or friends can rack up the most steps!

▸ Park farther away at the grocery store or mall and walk the extra distance. Even better—walk or bike to your destination instead of driving. Use stairs rather than the elevator whenever you can.

▸ Turn on the radio and have an inside dance party.

▸ Can't miss your favorite television show? Use a stationary bike or treadmill while you're watching. If you don't have the space or equipment to make that a reality, walk in place, lift weights, or do floor exercises like planks, crunches, and leg lifts.

- Use something you have around the house—a can of beans, a full water bottle—to do simple arm exercises like bicep curls.

- Do squats when you're putting away groceries or picking up your children.

- Need to straighten up around the house? Set the timer for small bursts of activity—even five or ten minutes of vigorous cleaning will get you moving.

- Plan active vacations, rather than driving trips. Walk the streets of an unfamiliar city, or enjoy nature by hiking, canoeing, or cycling.

Movement at Work

Many of the same ideas apply if your work keeps you sitting still most of the day:

- If you park in a deck or garage, find a space at the far end so you have farther to walk. If you take transit, get off one stop early and walk the extra distance. If you can, use the stairs or escalator instead of the elevator.

- Stuck sitting at conference tables? Have a walking meeting. Instead of e-mailing your coworker down the hall, walk to her office to deliver a message. Use the bathroom that's farthest from your desk.

- At your desk, try sitting on an exercise ball instead of a regular desk chair. Stand up and pace during conference calls, or stay seated and do leg lifts, knee lifts, and toe curls. If you have a wall, do standing push-ups. If you're feeling adventurous, keep a weight under your desk for bicep curls.

- Exercise at lunch with workmates. Or walk on your own while you listen to music or an interesting podcast or book.

- When you need a break, stretch or take a quick walk instead of going online or gossiping with a coworker.

NOTES

REFERENCES

1. US Food and Drug Administration. Guidance for industry: a food labeling guide (16. Appendix H: Rounding the values according to FDA rounding rules). http://www. fda.gov/Food/GuidanceRegulation/GuidanceDocuments-RegulatoryInformation/LabelingNutrition/ucm064932. htm. Revised June 24, 2015. Accessed April 27, 2016.

2. Kushi, LH, Doyle C, McCullough M, Rock CL, Demark-Wahnefried W, Bandera EV, Gapstur S, Patel AV, Andrews K, Gansler T, The American Cancer Society 2010 Nutrition and Physical Activity Guidelines Advisory Committee (2012). American Cancer Society guidelines on nutrition and physical activity for cancer prevention. *CA Cancer J Clin.* 2012; 62(1):30–67. doi: 10.3322/caac.20140

3. Wolfson JA, Bleich SN. Is cooking at home associated with better diet quality or weight-loss intention? *Public Health Nutr.* 2015; 18(8):1397–1406 doi:10.1017/S1368980014001943. Epub 2014 Nov 17.

4. World Cancer Research Fund/American Institute for Cancer Research. *Food, Nutrition, Physical Activity, and the Prevention of Cancer: a Global Perspective.* Washington DC: AICR, 2007.

5. Bernstein AM, Sun Q, Hu FB, Stampfer MJ, Manson JE, Willett WC. Major dietary protein sources and risk of coronary heart disease in women. *Circulation.* 2010; 122(9):876–883. doi:10.1161/ CIRCULATIONAHA.109.915165. Epub 2010 Aug 16.

6. Aune D, Ursin G, Veierød MB. Meat consumption and the risk of type 2 diabetes; a systematic review and meta-analysis of cohort studies. *Diabetologia.* 2009; 52(11):2277–2287. doi:10.1007/s00125-009-1481-x. Epub 2009 Aug 7.

7. Pan A, Sun Q, Bernstein AM, Schulze MB, Manson JE, Stampfer MJ, Willett WC, Hu FB. Red meat consumption and mortality: results from 2 prospective cohort studies. *Arch Intern Med.* 2012; 172(7):555–563. doi:10.1001/archinternmed.2011.2287. Epub 2012 Mar 12.

8. Pan A, Sun Q, Bernstein AM, Schulze MB, Manson JE, Willett WC, Hu FB. Red meat consumption and risk of type 2 diabetes: 3 cohorts of US adults and an updated meta-analysis. *Am J Clin Nutr.* 2011;94(4):1088–1096. doi:10.2945/ajch.111.018978. Epub 2011 Aug 10.

9. Bernstein AM, Pan A, Rexrode KM, Stampfer M, Hu FB, Mozaffarian D, Willett WC. Dietary protein sources and the risk of stroke in men and women. *Stroke.* 2012; 43(3): 637–644. doi:10.1161/STROKEAHA.111.633404. Epub 2011 Dec 29.

10. Manson JE, Bassuk SS. The type of fat you eat matters! Harvard Health Blog. http://www.health.harvard.edu/blog/ the-type-of-fat-you-eat-matters-201509228333. Published September 22, 2015. Accessed May 6, 2016.

11. Hu FB, Stampfer MJ, Manson JE, Rimm E, Colditz GA, Rosner BA, Hennekens CH, Willett WC. Dietary fat intake and the risk of coronary heart disease in women. *N Engl J Med.* 1997; 337(21):1491–1499.

12. Ascherio A, Rimm EB, Giovannucci EL, Spiegelman D, Meir S, Willett WC. Dietary fat and risk of coronary heart disease in men: cohort follow up study in the United States. *BMJ.* 1996; 313:84–90. doi:http://dx.doi.org/10.1136/ bmj.313.7049.84

13. Siri-Tarino PW, Sun Q, Hu FB, Krauss RM. Saturated fatty acids and risk of coronary heart disease: modulation by replacement nutrients. *Curr Atheroscler Rep.* 2010; 12(6):384–390. doi:10.1007/s11883-010-0131-6. Epub 2010 Aug 14.

14. Astrup A, Dyerberg J, Elwood P, Hermansen K, Hu FB, Jakobsen MU, Kok FJ, Krauss RM, Lecerf JM, LeGrand P, Nestel P, Risérus U, Sanders T, Sinclair A, Stender S, Tholstrup T, Willett WC. The role of reducing intakes of saturated fat in the prevention of cardiovascular disease: where does the evidence stand in 2010? *Am J Clin Nutr.* 2011; 93(4): 684–688.

15. Farvid MS, Ding M, Pan A, Sun Q, Chiuve SE, Steffen LM, Willett WC, Hu FB. Dietary linoleic acid and risk of coronary heart disease: a systematic review and meta-analysis of prospective cohort studies. *Circulation.* 2014; 130(18):1568–1578. doi:10.1161/CIRCULATION AHA.114.010236.

16. Mozaffarian D, Micha R, Wallace S. Effects on coronary heart disease of increasing polyunsaturated fat in place of saturated fat: a systematic review and meta-analysis of randomized controlled trials. *PLoS Med.* 2010; 7(3):1–10. doi:10.1371/journal.pmed.1000252.

17. Kratz M. Dietary cholesterol, atherosclerosis and coronary heart disease. *Handb Exp Pharmacol.* 2005; (170): 195–213.

18. Hu FB, Stampfer MJ, Rimm EB, Manson JE, Ascherio A, Colditz GA, Rosner BA, Spiegelman D, Speizer FE, Sacks FM, Hennekens CH, Willett WC. A prospective study of egg consumption and risk of cardiovascular disease in men and women. *JAMA.*1999; 281(15):1387–1394.

19. Thorning TK, Raziani F, Bendsen NT, Astrup A, Tholstrup, Raben A. Diets with high-fat cheese, high-fat meat, or carbohydrate on cardiovascular risk markers in overweight postmenopausal women: a randomized crossover trial. *Am J Clin Nutr.* 2015; 102(3):573–581.

20. Bertoia ML, Mukamal KJ, Cahill LE, Hou T, Ludwig DS, Mozaffarian D, Willett WC, Hu FB, Rimm EB. Changes in intake of fruits and vegetables and weight change in United States men and women followed for up to 24 years: analysis from three prospective cohort studies. *PLoS Med.* 2015; 12(9). doi:10.1371/journal.pmed.1001878.

21. Jackson SL, King SM, Zhao L, Cogswell ME. Prevalence of excess sodium intake in the United States – NHANES. 2009–2012. *MMWR Morb Mortal Wkly Rep.* 2016; 64(52):1393–1397. doi:10.15585/mmwr.mm6452a1.

22. US Department of Health and Human Services/ Centers for Disease Control and Prevention. New Research: Excess sodium intake remains common in the United States. Press Release. January 7, 2016: http://www.cdc.gov/media/releases/2016/p0106-sodium-intake.html.

23. Johnson RK, Appel LJ, Brands M, Howard BV, Lefevre M, Lustig RH, Sacks F, Steffen LM, Wylie-Rosett J. Dietary sugars intake and cardiovascular health: a scientific statement from the American Heart Association. *Circulation.* 2009; 120:1011–1120. doi:10.1161/CIRCULATIONAHA.109.192627.

24. Ogden CL, Carroll MD, Kit BK, Flegal KM. Prevalence of obesity and trends in body mass index among US children and adolescents, 1999–2010. *JAMA.* 2012; 307(5): 483–490. doi: 10.1001/jama.2012.40. Epub 2012 Jan 17.

25. Flegal KM, Carroll MD, Kit BK, Ogden CL. Prevalence of obesity and trends in the distribution of body mass index among US adults, 1999–2010. *JAMA.* 2012; 307(5):491–497. doi: 10.1001/jama.2012.39. Epub 2012 Jan 17.

26. Malik VS, Popkin BM, Bray GA, Després JP, Willett WC, Hu FB. Sugar-sweetened beverages and risk of metabolic syndrome and type 2 diabetes: a meta-analysis. *Diabetes Care.* 2010; 33(11):2477–2483.

27. de Koning L, Malik VS, Kellogg MD, Rimm EB, Willett WC, Hu FB. Sweetened beverage consumption, incident coronary heart disease, and biomarkers of risk in men. *Circulation.* 2012; 125:1735–1741, S1. doi:10.1161/ CIRCULATIONAHA.111.067017.

28. Fung TT, Malik V, Rexrode KM, Manson JE, Willett WC, Hu FB. Sweetened beverage consumption and risk of coronary heart disease in women. *Am J Clin Nutr.* 2009; 89(4):1037–1042.

29. Choi HK, Willett W, Curhan G. Fructose-rich beverages and risk of gout in women. *JAMA.* 2010; 304(20):2270–2278. doi:10.1001/jama.2010.1638. Epub 2010 Nov 10.

30. Choi HK, Curhan G. Soft drinks, fructose consumption, and the risk of gout in men: prospective cohort study. *BMJ.* 2008; 336(7639):309–312. doi:10.1136/ bmj.39449.819271.BE. Epub 2008 Jan 31.

31. Ebbeling CB, Feldman HA, Osganian SK, Chomitz VR, Ellenbogen SJ, Ludwig DS. Effects of decreasing sugar-sweetened beverage consumption on body weight in adolescents: a randomized, controlled pilot study. *Pediatrics.* 2006; 117(3):673–680. doi:10.1542/ peds.2005-0983.

32. Tate DF, Turner-McGrievy G, Lyons E, Stevens J, Erickson K, Polzien K, Diamond M, Wang X, Popkin B. Replacing caloric beverages with water or diet beverages for weight loss in adults: main results of the Choose Healthy Options Consciously Everyday (CHOICE) randomized clinical trial. *Am J Clin Nutr.* 2012; 95(3):555–563.

33. US Department of Agriculture. Nutrient data for 14400, Carbonated beverage, cola, contains caffeine. National Nutrient Database for Standard Reference, Release 24. 2012. Accessed June 21, 2012. http://ndb.nal. usda.gov/ndb/foods/show/4337.

34. The Coca-Cola Company. History of bottling. http:// www.coca-colacompany.com/our-company/history-of-bottling/. Accessed May 4, 2016.

35. Jacobson M. Liquid candy: how soft drinks are harming Americans' health. Washington, DC: Center for Science in the Public Interest; 2005; 1–35.

36. The Coca-Cola Company. New 1.25 liter Coca-Cola package rolls out as part of brand's 125th Anniversary celebration. http://www.bevnet.com/news/2011/new-1-25-liter-coca-cola-package-rolls-out-as-part-of-brands-125th-anniversary-celebration. Accessed May 4, 2016.

37. Institute of Medicine of the National Academies. *Accelerating Progress in Obesity Prevention: Solving the Weight of the Nation.* Washington, DC, May 2012. ©2012 by the National Academy of Sciences.

38. Pan A, Hu FB. Effects of carbohydrates on satiety: differences between liquid and solid food. *Curr Opin Clin Nutr Metab Care.* 2011; 14(4):385–390. doi:10.1097/MCO.0b013e328346df36.

39. Anderson E, Shivakumar G. Effects of exercise and physical activity on anxiety. **Front Psychiatry.** 2013; 4(27):1–4. doi:10.3389/fpsyt.2013.00027.

40. US Department of Health and Human Services/Office of Disease Prevention and Health Promotion. *2008 Physical Activity Guidelines for Americans.* http://health.gov/paguidelines/guidelines/ Revised May 5, 2016. Accessed May 5, 2016.

41. Hunter GR, McCarthy JP, Bamman MM. Effects of resistance training on older adults. *Sports Med.* 2004; 34(5):329–348.

42. Williams MA, Haskell WL, Ades PH, Amsterdam EA, Bittner V, Franklin BA, Gulanick M, Laing ST, Stewart KJ. Resistance exercise in individuals with and without cardiovascular disease: 2007 update. A Scientific Statement from the American Heart Association Council on Clinical Cardiology and Council on Nutrition, Physical Activity, and Metabolism. *Circulation.* 2007; 116(5):572–584. doi:10.1161/CIRCULATIONAHA.107.185214

43. Engelke K, Kemmler W, Lauber D, Beeskow C, Pintag R, Kalendar WA. Exercise maintains bone density at spine and hip EFOPS: a 3-year longitudinal study in early post-menopausal women. *Osteoporos Int.* 2006; 17(1):133–142. Epub 2005 Aug 12.

44. Katzmarzyk, PT, Craig CL. Musculoskeletal fitness and risk of mortality. *Med Sci Sports Exerc.* 2002; 34(5):740–744.

45. Gale CR, Martyn CN, Cooper C, Sayer AA. Grip strength, body composition, and mortality. *Int J Epidemiol.* 2007; 36(1):228–235. Epub 2006 Oct 19.

46. Bohannon RW. Hand-grip dynamometry predicts future outcomes in aging adults. *J Geriatr Phys Ther.* 2008; 31(1):3–10.

47. Ling CHY, Taekema D, de Craen AJM, Gusselkloo J, Westendorp RGJ, Maier AB. Handgrip strength and mortality in the oldest old population: the Leiden 85-plus study. *CMAJ.* 2010; 182(5):429–435. doi:10.1503/cmaj.091278

48. Ruiz JR, Sui X, Lobelo F, Morrow JR, Jackson AW, Sjostrom M, Blair SN. Association between muscular strength and mortality in men: prospective cohort study. *BMJ.* 2008; 337:a439.

41. Hunter GR, McCarthy JP, Bamman MM. Effects of resistance training on older adults. *Sports Med.* 2004; 34(5):329–348.

42. Williams MA, Haskell WL, Ades PH, Amsterdam EA, Bittner V, Franklin BA, Gulanick M, Laing ST, Stewart KJ. Resistance exercise in individuals with and without cardiovascular disease: 2007 update. A Scientific Statement from the American Heart Association Council on Clinical Cardiology and Council on Nutrition, Physical Activity, and Metabolism. *Circulation.* 2007; 116(5):572–584. doi:10.1161/ CIRCULATIONAHA.107.185214

43. Engelke K, Kemmler W, Lauber D, Beeskow C, Pintag R, Kalendar WA. Exercise maintains bone density at spine and hip EFOPS: a 3-year longitudinal study in early postmenopausal women. *Osteoporos Int.* 2006; 17(1):133–142. Epub 2005 Aug 12.

44. Katzmarzyk, PT, Craig CL. Musculoskeletal fitness and risk of mortality. *Med Sci Sports Exerc.* 2002; 34(5):740–744.

45. Gale CR, Martyn CN, Cooper C, Sayer AA. Grip strength, body composition, and mortality. *Int J Epidemiol.* 2007; 36(1):228–235. Epub 2006 Oct 19.

46. Bohannon RW. Hand-grip dynamometry predicts future outcomes in aging adults. *J Geriatr Phys Ther.* 2008; 31(1):3–10.

47. Ling CHY, Taekema D, de Craen AJM, Gusselkloo J, Westendorp RGJ, Maier AB. Handgrip strength and mortality in the oldest old population: the Leiden 85-plus study. *CMAJ.* 2010; 182(5):429–435. doi:10.1503/cmaj.091278

48. Ruiz JR, Sui X, Lobelo F, Morrow JR, Jackson AW, Sjostrom M, Blair SN. Association between muscular strength and mortality in men: prospective cohort study. *BMJ.* 2008; 337:a439.

MAIN COURSES

PEANUT NOODLES WITH SNOW PEAS AND BROCCOLI

When you want all the flavor of takeout noodles but with more vegetables and a lot less oil and sugar, try this version. The spicy peanut sauce coats noodles, broccoli, carrots, and snow peas for a delicious at-home meal with restaurant flavor. For a milder flavor, blanch the garlic in the boiling water before you cook the pasta. Just drop the cloves in for twenty seconds, then remove them and process as described.

6 TO 8 SERVINGS

8 ounces linguine, spaghetti, or soba noodles

1 cup small broccoli florets

1 cup snow peas, trimmed and sliced horizontally

1 carrot, shredded

2 garlic cloves

1 (1-inch) piece peeled fresh ginger, coarsely chopped

1/2 cup peanut butter, preferably all natural

1/4 cup plus 1 tablespoon reduced-sodium soy sauce

3 tablespoons dark sesame oil

2 tablespoons unseasoned rice vinegar

1 tablespoon honey

2 teaspoons chili garlic sauce

2 cups shredded cooked chicken breast, optional

Prepare the linguine according to the package directions for al dente (just firm). About 2 minutes before the pasta is ready, add the broccoli, snow peas, and carrot. Reserve 1/4 cup of the pasta water before draining.

Meanwhile, in a food processor with the motor running, add the garlic and ginger. Scrape down the sides and add the peanut butter, soy sauce, sesame oil, vinegar, honey, and chili garlic sauce and process until smooth.

In a bowl, combine the sauce and pasta mixture and stir to combine (if too dry, add a tablespoon or so of reserved cooking liquid). Add the chicken, if desired, and stir to combine.

PER SERVING

Calories	390
Calories from fat	170
Fat	19 g
Saturated fat	3 g
Trans fatty acids, total	0 g
Polyunsaturated fat	7 g
Monounsaturated fat	8 g
Cholesterol	0 mg
Sodium	510 mg
Carbohydrate	42 g
Dietary fiber	4 g
Sugars	7 g
Protein	12 g

 For a more substantial dish, add two cups of cooked chicken (if you have leftovers from a store-bought or homemade roasted bird). If you can't find chili garlic sauce, substitute chili paste (sambal oelek) or Sriracha.

CHICKEN WITH MARSALA AND WILD MUSHROOMS

In this version of a classic Italian entrée, chicken is sautéed with wild mushrooms and coated with a luscious wine sauce reduction. When making a sauce like this one, don't use a nonstick pan, and take care not to overcrowd the pan; you want the breasts to brown, not steam in their own juices. You might need to cook the chicken in batches.

4 SERVINGS

1/4 cup all-purpose flour

1/4 teaspoon salt

1/4 teaspoon freshly ground black pepper

1 pound boneless, skinless chicken breasts, pounded or sliced to even thickness

2 tablespoons olive oil, divided use

1 shallot, minced

8 ounces mushrooms (wild, white, or a combination), sliced

1/4 teaspoon dried thyme

3/4 cup Marsala wine

3/4 cup reduced-sodium chicken broth

On a plate, combine the flour, salt, and pepper. Add the chicken and coat with flour.

In a large skillet over medium-high heat, add 1 tablespoon of the oil. Cook the chicken for 3 to 4 minutes per side, or until just cooked through and golden brown. Remove the chicken and set aside. Add the remaining 1 tablespoon of oil, and sauté the shallot for 1 minute. Add the mushrooms and thyme and sauté for 5 to 8 minutes, or until softened. Add the Marsala and broth and boil until the sauce thickens and reduces by half, stirring to dislodge any bits of food that have stuck to the bottom of the skillet. Reduce the heat to medium-low, return the chicken and any accumulated juices to the skillet, and cook for 1 to 2 minutes, or until the chicken is heated through and coated with sauce.

PER SERVING

Calories	270
Calories from fat	90
Fat	10 g
Saturated fat	2 g
Trans fatty acids, total	0 g
Polyunsaturated fat	1.5 g
Monounsaturated fat	6 g
Cholesterol	65 mg
Sodium	230 mg
Carbohydrate	12 g
Dietary fiber	2 g
Sugars	2 g
Protein	27 g

Marsala is a fortified wine, like port or sherry. It is produced in the area around Marsala, Sicily.

LENTIL AND EGGPLANT STEW WITH APRICOTS

This version of the traditional Armenian dish vospapur, a hearty vegetarian stew, is filled with protein- and nutrient-rich lentils, as well as eggplant, tomatoes, spices, fresh herbs, and an unexpected ingredient—dried apricots. If you have spinach on hand, add a few cups to the dish just before serving. If you prefer stronger flavors, increase the spices to your liking.

If you are watching your sodium intake, choose no-salt-added tomatoes and substitute homemade broth (page 206) for store-bought.

4 TO 6 SERVINGS

1 cup brown lentils

4 cups reduced-sodium chicken or vegetable broth

1/2 cup quartered dried apricots

2 tablespoons olive oil

1 onion, chopped

1 red bell pepper, seeded and coarsely chopped

1 pound eggplant, peeled and coarsely chopped

3 garlic cloves, minced

2 teaspoons paprika

1/2 teaspoon ground cinnamon

1/4 teaspoon ground allspice

1/4 teaspoon cayenne pepper

1 (28-ounce) can diced tomatoes

1/4 cup chopped fresh Italian parsley

2 tablespoons chopped fresh mint

Salt and freshly ground black pepper

In a stockpot over medium-high heat, combine the lentils and broth and bring to a boil. Reduce the heat, cover, and simmer for 15 minutes. Add the apricots and stir to combine.

Meanwhile, in a large skillet over medium-high heat, add the oil. Sauté the onion for 3 to 5 minutes, or until softened. Add the bell pepper and eggplant and sauté for 5 minutes. Add the garlic, paprika, cinnamon, allspice, and cayenne pepper and sauté for 1 minute. Add the tomatoes and their juice and bring to a boil. Reduce the heat and simmer for 10 minutes, or until thickened, stirring occasionally. Add the tomato mixture to the lentils and simmer for 15 minutes. Add the parsley and mint. Season with salt and pepper.

PER SERVING

Calories	370
Calories from fat	70
Fat	8 g
Saturated fat	1 g
Trans fatty acids, total	0 g
Polyunsaturated fat	1.5 g
Monounsaturated fat	5 g
Cholesterol	0 mg
Sodium	810 mg
Carbohydrate	61 g
Dietary fiber	20 g
Sugars	24 g
Protein	19 g

 TIP *Onions and bell peppers contain a lot of water. If you use a food processor to chop them, use the pulse button to control the blade so you don't accidentally overdo it and turn them into pulp.*

STUFFED PEPPERS WITH TURKEY AND OLIVES

Colorful bell peppers are the perfect vessels for this Spanish-inspired filling. In this recipe, ground turkey breast is studded with crunchy almonds, toothsome currants, and briny olives. You can find roasted almonds in many stores, either in self-serve bins or packages. If you can't find them, toast the almonds in a 350-degree oven for eight to twelve minutes, or until they are golden and fragrant, stirring often to prevent burning.

4 SERVINGS

4 large red, orange, green, or yellow bell peppers

1 tablespoon olive oil

3/4 pound ground turkey breast

4 scallions, white and light green parts only, thinly sliced

2 garlic cloves, minced

1/4 teaspoon ground cinnamon

1/4 teaspoon ground cloves

1 teaspoon crushed red pepper flakes

1 (8-ounce) can tomato sauce

1 cup cooked brown or white rice or other grain

1/2 cup currants

1/3 cup chopped green olives

1/3 cup chopped toasted almonds

Salt and freshly ground black pepper

Preheat the oven to 350 degrees.

Cut off the tops of the peppers and carefully remove the seeds and large membranes. Slice a thin strip off the bottom of each bell pepper so it can stand upright. Place the peppers in a steamer rack over boiling water. Cover and cook for 5 minutes. Transfer the peppers to a baking pan.

Meanwhile, in a large skillet over medium-high heat, add the oil. Sauté the turkey and scallions for 5 to 8 minutes, or until the turkey is cooked through. Add the garlic, cinnamon, cloves, and red pepper flakes and sauté for 1 minute. Add the tomato sauce, reduce the heat, and simmer, stirring to combine. Add the rice, currants, olives, and almonds and stir to combine. Season with salt and pepper.

Spoon the turkey mixture into the peppers. Bake for 20 to 25 minutes, or until heated through.

PER SERVING

Calories	390
Calories from fat	110
Fat	12 g
Saturated fat	2 g
Trans fatty acids, total	0 g
Polyunsaturated fat	2.5 g
Monounsaturated fat	7 g
Cholesterol	50 mg
Sodium	520 mg
Carbohydrate	44 g
Dietary fiber	9 g
Sugars	25 g
Protein	28 g

Make this recipe when you have leftover rice from a prior night, or mix in whatever cooked grain you have on hand: rice, quinoa, and farro are other good options. Even quick-cooking couscous would work well.

FUSILLI WITH BROCCOLI AND DECONSTRUCTED PESTO

This recipe presents the ingredients found in pesto in a fresh, less muddled way. Instead of blending herbs, nuts, and cheese into a paste, here they are left in their individual states so the flavors sing.

There are other advantages to this preparation: cooking the garlic mellows it without losing its punch, and adding a little chicken broth replaces some of the oil traditionally used to make pesto.

4 SERVINGS

- 8 ounces fusilli or other shaped pasta
- 12 ounces small broccoli florets
- 2 tablespoons olive oil
- 5 garlic cloves, minced

- 1/2 cup reduced-sodium chicken or vegetable broth
- 3/4 cup chopped fresh basil
- 1/2 cup chopped fresh Italian parsley
- 2 tablespoons extra-virgin olive oil

- 1/4 cup freshly grated Parmesan cheese
- 2 tablespoons pine nuts, toasted
- Salt and freshly ground black pepper

Prepare the fusilli according to the package directions for al dente (just firm). About 2 minutes before the pasta is ready, add the broccoli. Reserve 1/4 cup of the pasta water before draining.

Meanwhile, in a large skillet over medium heat, add the olive oil. Sauté the garlic for 1 minute. Add the broth and bring to a boil for 3 to 5 minutes, or until reduced by half, stirring frequently. Reduce the heat, add the pasta and broccoli, and stir until coated with sauce. Add the basil and parsley and stir to combine. Transfer to a bowl and drizzle with the extra-virgin olive oil (if too dry, add a tablespoon or so of reserved cooking liquid). Top with the cheese and pine nuts. Season with salt and pepper.

PER SERVING

Calories	400
Calories from fat	170
Fat	18 g
Saturated fat	3 g
Trans fatty acids, total	0 g
Polyunsaturated fat	4 g
Monounsaturated fat	11 g
Cholesterol	Less than 5 mg
Sodium	130 mg
Carbohydrate	48 g
Dietary fiber	5 g
Sugars	4 g
Protein	12 g

Explore your local farmers markets. They often offer a wide variety of freshly picked, locally grown vegetables and herbs at reasonable prices.

PORTOBELLO AND POBLANO TACOS

Sometimes less is more, and that is particularly true in this tasty vegetarian meal that comes together in less than thirty minutes. For added protein, serve with a side of black beans or a bean salad. Give the mushrooms a quick rinse or wipe them with a wet paper towel, but be sure to dry them well to prevent sogginess.

4 SERVINGS

1 tablespoon canola oil

1 red onion, sliced

4 garlic cloves, minced

3 poblano peppers, halved, seeded, and sliced into strips

3 portobello mushrooms, stemmed and sliced

8 ounces cremini (baby bella), shiitake, or white mushrooms, thinly sliced

2 teaspoons ground cumin

1 teaspoon dried oregano

Salt and freshly ground black pepper

8 (5- to 6-inch) whole wheat, flour, or corn tortillas

1 avocado

1 tablespoon fresh lemon juice

1/2 cup shredded reduced-fat or regular Mexican-blend cheese or Cotija cheese

Sriracha or other hot sauce, optional

Chopped fresh cilantro, optional

Preheat the oven to 350 degrees.

In a large skillet over medium-high heat, add the oil. Sauté the onion for 3 to 5 minutes, or until softened. Add the garlic and sauté for 1 minute. Add the poblanos, mushrooms, cumin, and oregano and sauté for 5 to 8 minutes, or until the mushrooms have softened and released their liquid. Season with salt and pepper.

Meanwhile, wrap the tortillas in aluminum foil and bake for 10 minutes. (Tortillas can also be wrapped in a damp towel and warmed in the microwave on high for 15 to 30 seconds.)

In a bowl, coarsely mash the avocado and stir gently with lemon juice. Season with salt. Spread a heaping tablespoon on each tortilla. Top with the vegetables and 1 tablespoon of cheese. Add a squirt of Sriracha and a sprinkle of cilantro, if desired.

PER SERVING	
Calories	360
Calories from fat	160
Fat	18 g
Saturated fat	6 g
Trans fatty acids, total	0 g
Polyunsaturated fat	2.5 g
Monounsaturated fat	9 g
Cholesterol	10 mg
Sodium	390 mg
Carbohydrate	43 g
Dietary fiber	10 g
Sugars	8 g
Protein	14 g

CHICKEN-BLACK BEAN "TAMALE" CASSEROLE

This hearty casserole is chock-full of veggies, beans, and shredded chicken. Bake and serve this in any ovenproof dish that is eight-by-ten-inches or smaller, to ensure the crust covers the filling. The smaller the dish, the thicker the crust, so allow a few more minutes' cooking time.

4 SERVINGS

- 1 tablespoon canola oil
- 1 onion, chopped
- 1 red bell pepper, seeded and chopped
- 1 green bell pepper, seeded and chopped
- 1 jalapeño pepper, seeded and finely chopped
- 1 garlic clove, minced

- 2 teaspoons chili powder
- 1 teaspoon ground cumin
- 1 (14.5-ounce) can diced tomatoes
- 3 cups shredded cooked chicken breast
- 1 (15-ounce) can black beans, rinsed and drained

- 1 cup corn
- $1/2$ teaspoon salt
- 1 cup reduced-sodium chicken broth
- 1 cup water
- $3/4$ cup cornmeal
- 1 tablespoon butter

Preheat the oven to 375 degrees.

In a large skillet over medium heat, add the oil. Sauté the onion for 3 to 5 minutes. Add bell peppers and jalapeño and sauté for 3 minutes, or until softened. Add the garlic, chili powder, and cumin and sauté for 1 minute. Add the tomatoes and their juice and bring to a boil, stirring to combine. Reduce the heat and simmer for 5 to 10 minutes, or until thickened, stirring occasionally. Add the chicken, black beans, corn, and salt and cook for 5 minutes. Remove from the heat.

In a saucepan over medium-high heat, bring the broth and water to a simmer. Add the cornmeal, whisking constantly to incorporate. Continue to whisk for 5 minutes, or until the cornmeal thickens and pulls away from the edges and bottom of the pan. Remove from the heat and whisk in the butter.

Transfer the chicken mixture to an 8-by-10-inch (or slightly smaller) casserole dish or baking pan and spread the cornmeal mixture over the top. Bake for 20 to 30 minutes, or until the top firms up. Let rest for 5 to 10 minutes before serving.

PER SERVING

Calories	500
Calories from fat	110
Fat	12 g
Saturated fat	3.5 g
Trans fatty acids, total	0 g
Polyunsaturated fat	2.5 g
Monounsaturated fat	4.5 g
Cholesterol	95 mg
Sodium	740 mg
Carbohydrate	56 g
Dietary fiber	11 g
Sugars	10 g
Protein	44 g

For more spice, substitute canned tomatoes with chilies for the plain diced tomatoes or add a few shakes of hot sauce. For a vegetarian version, use vegetable stock and substitute portobello mushrooms or your favorite type of winter squash for the chicken. If you are feeling "cheesy," mix $3/4$ cup shredded sharp Cheddar cheese into the cornmeal mixture before baking.

ROASTED BUTTERNUT SQUASH AND BARLEY STEW

Roasting the squash separately allows it to caramelize and prevents it from overcooking in the stew. Adding the rind from a piece of Parmesan cheese lends subtle flavor. If you have fresh dill on hand, sprinkle a little on top before serving.

You might need to use two baking sheets to fit all of the squash in a single layer.

6 SERVINGS

- 1 butternut squash (about 2 pounds), peeled, seeded, and cut into 3/4-inch cubes
- 2 tablespoons canola oil, divided use
- Salt and freshly ground black pepper
- 2 carrots, chopped
- 1 onion, chopped
- 1 celery stalk, chopped
- 8 ounces white mushrooms, sliced
- 2 garlic cloves, minced
- 5 cups reduced-sodium chicken or vegetable broth
- 1 cup pearl barley
- 1 (2-inch piece) Parmesan cheese rind, optional
- 2 cups fresh baby spinach
- 1 tablespoon chopped fresh dill, optional

Preheat the oven to 400 degrees.

Lightly coat a foil-lined, rimmed baking sheet with nonstick cooking spray. Place the squash on the baking sheet and drizzle with 1 tablespoon of the oil. Sprinkle with salt and pepper and stir to combine. Evenly distribute the squash on the baking sheet. Roast for 20 to 30 minutes, or until tender and slightly charred, stirring the squash every 10 minutes.

Meanwhile, in a stockpot over medium-high heat, add the remaining 1 tablespoon of oil. Sauté the carrots, onion, and celery for 5 to 8 minutes, or until softened. Add the mushrooms and garlic and sauté for 5 minutes. Add the broth and bring to a boil. Add the barley and Parmesan rind and stir to combine. Reduce the heat, cover, and simmer for 35 to 45 minutes, or until the barley is tender, stirring occasionally. Add the spinach and stir until wilted. Add the butternut squash (and dill, if desired), and stir to combine. Season with salt and pepper.

PER SERVING

Calories	205
Calories from fat	50
Fat	6 g
Saturated fat	0 g
Trans fatty acids, total	0 g
Polyunsaturated fat	1.5 g
Monounsaturated fat	3 g
Cholesterol	0 mg
Sodium	460 mg
Carbohydrate	35 g
Dietary fiber	7 g
Sugars	5 g
Protein	7 g

PEANUT CHICKEN SKEWERS

With a slightly spiced peanut butter marinade similar to satay, the Thai restaurant mainstay, these chicken skewers are destined to be a family favorite. Marinate them ahead of time and then broil or cook on a stovetop or outdoor grill. They'll be ready in the time it takes to set the table!

Serve with rice and Sweet and Sour Cucumber Salad (page 153) for a refreshing dinner.

4 SERVINGS

1/3 cup peanut butter, preferably all natural

1/4 small red onion or 1 small shallot, chopped

1 garlic clove

1 (1-inch) piece peeled fresh ginger, coarsely chopped

2 tablespoons rice vinegar or white vinegar

2 teaspoons reduced-sodium soy sauce

Juice of 1/2 lemon

1/2 teaspoon ground cumin

1/2 teaspoon curry powder

1 pound boneless, skinless chicken breasts, cut into 1-inch pieces

In a food processor, combine the peanut butter, onion, garlic, ginger, vinegar, soy sauce, lemon juice, cumin, and curry powder until smooth. The mixture will be thick. Transfer to a zip-top bag or bowl. Add the chicken and turn to coat. Refrigerate for 3 or more hours, turning occasionally if possible.

Preheat the broiler to high and set an oven rack 3 to 4 inches from the heat. Lightly coat a foil-lined, rimmed baking sheet or broiler pan with nonstick cooking spray.

Remove the chicken from the marinade, letting excess drip off. Thread on skewers and place on the baking sheet. Broil the chicken for 5 to 7 minutes, or until just cooked through, turning every 1 to 2 minutes.

PER SERVING

Calories	160
Calories from fat	45
Fat	5.0 g
Saturated fat	1 g
Trans fatty acids, total	0 g
Polyunsaturated fat	1.5 g
Monounsaturated fat	2 g
Cholesterol	65 mg
Sodium	75 mg
Carbohydrate	1 g
Dietary fiber	0 g
Sugars	0 g
Protein	25 g

TIP *If using wooden skewers, soak them in water while the chicken marinates to keep them from burning.*

ZESTY FISH TACOS WITH AVOCADO

Tilapia, affordable and readily available, is a favorite fish for these tacos. Feel free to enhance the taco by tucking in fresh or pickled jalapeño slices for heat. Serve with Honey Coleslaw (page 146) or add shredded cabbage or lettuce to the taco for crunch.

4 SERVINGS

4 (4- to 6-ounce) tilapia fillets

2 tablespoons "Mexican" or "Southwest" seasoning blend

Salt and freshly ground black pepper

1 tablespoon canola oil

8 (5- to 6-inch) whole wheat, flour, or corn tortillas

1/2 cup salsa

2 tablespoons regular or reduced-fat sour cream

1 avocado, cut into eight slices

1 lime or lemon, cut into eight wedges

Preheat the oven to 350 degrees.

Coat the tilapia with the seasoning blend. Season with salt and pepper.

In a large, preferably nonstick, skillet over medium-high heat, add the oil. Cook the tilapia for 2 to 4 minutes per side, or until just cooked through. When opaque, break up the fish with a spatula into 1- to 2-inch pieces.

Meanwhile, wrap the tortillas in aluminum foil and bake for 10 minutes. (Tortillas can also be wrapped in a damp towel and warmed in the microwave on high for 15 to 30 seconds.)

In a bowl, combine the salsa and sour cream. Spread a heaping tablespoon on each tortilla. Top with a few pieces of fish, a slice of avocado, and a squirt of lime.

PER SERVING

Calories	400
Calories from fat	160
Fat	18 g
Saturated fat	5 g
Trans fatty acids, total	0 g
Polyunsaturated fat	3 g
Monounsaturated fat	9 g
Cholesterol	55 mg
Sodium	530 mg
Carbohydrate	33 g
Dietary fiber	9 g
Sugars	3 g
Protein	29 g

 TIP *A silicone brush is helpful for spreading the oil evenly in the skillet.*

RICE NOODLES WITH SHRIMP, BOK CHOY, AND MINT

Using rice noodles instead of pasta makes this a great gluten-free option, although angel hair pasta works well, too. Drain the noodles well before mixing them with the vegetables so they don't dilute the sauce.

The noodles and the vegetable mixture cook very quickly, so make sure to have your veggies prepped and ready to go before starting to cook.

4 SERVINGS

- 6 ounces thin rice noodles
- 1/4 cup reduced-sodium soy sauce
- 3 tablespoons rice vinegar
- 3 tablespoons hoisin sauce
- 1 tablespoon canola oil
- 2 garlic cloves, minced
- 1 small jalapeño pepper, seeded and chopped
- 1 (2-inch) piece peeled fresh ginger, minced
- 3/4 pound shrimp, peeled and deveined
- 2 scallions, white and light green parts only, thinly sliced
- 2 carrots, shredded, or 1 cup packaged, shredded or "matchstick" carrots
- 1 red bell pepper, seeded and cut into thin strips
- 1 head bok choy, cored and thinly sliced
- 1 tablespoon dark sesame oil
- 2 tablespoons chopped fresh mint
- 2 tablespoons chopped peanuts

Prepare the noodles according to the package directions. Drain well and pat dry.

Meanwhile, in a bowl, combine the soy sauce, vinegar, and hoisin sauce.

In a large skillet over medium-high heat, add the oil. Sauté the garlic, jalapeño, and ginger for 1 minute. Add the shrimp, scallions, carrots, bell pepper, and bok choy and sauté for 2 to 3 minutes, or until the vegetables soften and the colors are vivid. Add the noodles and stir to combine. Add the sauce and stir to combine. Transfer to a serving bowl, drizzle with the sesame oil, and top with the mint and peanuts.

PER SERVING

Calories	440
Calories from fat	100
Fat	12 g
Saturated fat	1.5 g
Trans fatty acids, total	0 g
Polyunsaturated fat	4 g
Monounsaturated fat	5 g
Cholesterol	140 mg
Sodium	1280 mg
Carbohydrate	57 g
Dietary fiber	6 g
Sugars	10 g
Protein	28 g

If you don't have a jalapeño on hand, add chili garlic sauce, chili paste (sambal oelek), or crushed red pepper flakes, to taste. If you are watching your sodium intake, start with three tablespoons of soy sauce and two tablespoons of hoisin sauce. Add more to taste, if needed.

PASTA WITH EGGPLANT AND TOMATO SAUCE

This recipe is designed for the multitasker. While the water boils for the pasta, the tomato sauce is simmering on the stovetop and the eggplant is roasting in the oven. The caramelized eggplant adds heft to the topping, which holds up to the whole wheat pasta. Pick your favorite pasta shape.

4 SERVINGS

1 pound eggplant, cut into 1-inch pieces

3 tablespoons olive oil, divided use

1 onion, chopped

3 garlic cloves, minced

1/4 teaspoon crushed red pepper flakes

1 (28-ounce) can diced tomatoes

12 ounces whole wheat penne or other shaped pasta

Salt and freshly ground black pepper

Freshly grated Parmesan cheese, optional

Preheat the oven to 450 degrees.

Lightly coat a foil-lined, rimmed baking sheet with nonstick cooking spray. Place the eggplant on the baking sheet and drizzle with 1 tablespoon of the oil. Stir to combine. Evenly distribute the eggplant on the baking sheet. Roast for 20 to 25 minutes, or until tender and slightly charred, stirring the eggplant every 10 minutes.

In a large skillet over medium-high heat, add the remaining 2 tablespoons of oil. Sauté the onion, garlic, and red pepper flakes for 5 to 8 minutes, or until softened. Add the tomatoes and their juice and bring to a boil. Reduce the heat and simmer for 15 to 20 minutes, or until thickened, stirring occasionally.

Meanwhile, prepare the penne according to the package directions for al dente (just firm).

Add the eggplant to the tomato sauce and stir to combine. Season with salt and pepper. If there's room in the skillet, add the pasta to the sauce and stir to combine. If not, place the pasta in a bowl and add the sauce. Serve with cheese, if desired.

PER SERVING

Calories	490
Calories from fat	110
Fat	12 g
Saturated fat	2 g
Trans fatty acids, total	0 g
Polyunsaturated fat	2 g
Monounsaturated fat	8 g
Cholesterol	0 mg
Sodium	280 mg
Carbohydrate	87 g
Dietary fiber	14 g
Sugars	12 g
Protein	14 g

 TIP *There's no need to peel the eggplant before using. The same goes for carrots and potatoes. Just rinse them well.*

TURKEY-MUSHROOM MEATLOAF

Who doesn't love meatloaf? This version, made with heart-healthy turkey and finely chopped mushrooms instead of more caloric fillers, makes it even more loveable. Use a food processor to make the bread crumbs and then to finely chop the onion, garlic, and mushrooms.

4 TO 6 SERVINGS

TOPPING

1/4 cup ketchup

1 tablespoon light brown sugar

1/2 teaspoon dry mustard

MEATLOAF

1 egg

1 cup fresh bread crumbs (from 2 slices firm white sandwich bread, torn into small pieces)

1/2 cup low-fat milk

1 tablespoon canola oil

1 onion, finely chopped

3 garlic cloves, minced

8 ounces white or cremini mushrooms, finely chopped

3 tablespoons ketchup

1 tablespoon Worcestershire sauce

1 to 1 1/4 pounds ground turkey breast

Salt and freshly ground black pepper

FOR THE TOPPING: In a bowl, combine the ketchup, brown sugar, and mustard. Set aside.

FOR THE MEATLOAF: Preheat the oven to 400 degrees. Cut a piece of parchment paper into a 9-by-5-inch rectangle and place on a cooling rack on top of a foil-lined, rimmed baking sheet.

In a bowl, beat the egg. Add the bread crumbs and milk. Set aside to soften.

Meanwhile, in a large skillet over medium heat, add the oil. Sauté the onion for 5 to 8 minutes, or until softened. Add the garlic and sauté for 1 minute. Add the mushrooms and sauté for 5 to 8 minutes, or until they have softened and released all of their liquid. Set aside to cool briefly.

In a bowl, combine the bread crumb mixture, ketchup, and Worcestershire sauce. Add the

vegetable mixture and stir to combine. Add the turkey and stir gently to combine. Sprinkle with salt and pepper.

Form the turkey mixture into a loaf on top of the parchment and spread with the topping. Bake for 60 to 70 minutes, or until an instant-read thermometer inserted into the meatloaf registers 165 degrees. Let rest for 5 to 10 minutes before slicing.

PER SERVING

Calories	310
Calories from fat	70
Fat	8 g
Saturated fat	1.5 g
Trans fatty acids, total	0 g
Polyunsaturated fat	2.5 g
Monounsaturated fat	3.5 g
Cholesterol	135 mg
Sodium	540 mg
Carbohydrate	25 g
Dietary fiber	2 g
Sugars	15 g
Protein	35 g

TIP *A meatloaf sandwich is great for busy weeknights or to have on hand for lunch. Just tuck slices between bread; add lettuce, tomato, and a smear of mayo; and pack to take along with you.*

SEAFOOD AND SHELLFISH STEW

What could be more welcome on a chilly evening than a steaming bowl chock-full of fish and shellfish in a garlic, fennel, and tomato broth? Choose any firm white fish that looks good at the market: cod, sea bass, and halibut all work well. A thinner fillet, such as tilapia, will break apart in the stew but will still be delicious. If you can't find fennel, substitute a large celery stalk. If you only have small carrots, use two. For lower sodium, choose no-salt-added tomatoes. For a more soup-like consistency, add another bottle of clam juice.

4 SERVINGS

- 2 tablespoons olive oil
- 1 onion, finely chopped
- 1 large carrot, finely chopped
- 1 small fennel bulb, fronds and thick core removed, chopped
- 3 garlic cloves, minced
- 1 cup dry white wine
- 1 cup clam juice
- 1 (28-ounce) can diced tomatoes, drained
- 12 littleneck or small clams, scrubbed
- 12 mussels, scrubbed and debearded
- 1 pound firm white fish, cut into 1-inch pieces
- 12 shrimp, peeled and deveined
- Salt and freshly ground black pepper
- 2 tablespoons chopped fresh Italian parsley, optional

In a stockpot over medium heat, add the oil. Sauté the onion, carrot, and fennel for 8 to 10 minutes, or until softened. Add the garlic and sauté for 1 minute. Add the wine, clam juice, and tomatoes and bring to a boil, stirring to combine. Reduce the heat, cover, and simmer for 15 minutes, stirring occasionally. Add the clams and cook for 5 minutes. Add the mussels and cook for 3 minutes. Add the fish and cook for 1 minute. Add the shrimp and cook for 1 to 2 minutes, or until the seafood is just cooked through and the mussel and clam shells have opened. Season with salt and pepper. Sprinkle with parsley, if desired.

PER SERVING

Calories	320
Calories from fat	90
Fat	10 g
Saturated fat	0 g
Trans fatty acids, total	0 g
Polyunsaturated fat	1.5 g
Monounsaturated fat	5 g
Cholesterol	120 mg
Sodium	890 mg
Carbohydrate	16 g
Dietary fiber	3 g
Sugars	9 g
Protein	39 g

 TIP *The shells of clams and mussels should be tightly closed when you buy them. During cooking, if the clams or mussels open up before the rest of the seafood is done, remove them from the pot and add them back just before serving. If they take longer to open, serve the rest of the stew and continue to steam them in a cup of water until they open. Discard any that do not open.*

YOGURT- AND SPICE-INFUSED CHICKEN BREASTS

Marinating chicken in herbs, spices, and yogurt not only imparts flavor, it tenderizes the chicken. You can combine everything before work so it's ready to cook when you get home. Serve with Pearl Couscous "Tabbouleh" (page 126) or Sautéed Spinach with Raisins and Pine Nuts (page 137).

4 SERVINGS

½ cup nonfat plain Greek or regular yogurt

½ cup fresh cilantro

1 garlic clove

Juice of ½ lemon

1 (1-inch) piece peeled fresh ginger, coarsely chopped

¼ red onion or 1 shallot, coarsely chopped

½ teaspoon ground cumin

½ teaspoon kosher salt

½ teaspoon cayenne pepper

¼ teaspoon ground turmeric

1 pound boneless, skinless chicken breasts, pounded or sliced to even thickness

In a food processor, combine the yogurt, cilantro, garlic, lemon juice, ginger, onion, cumin, salt, cayenne pepper, and turmeric. Transfer to a zip-top bag or bowl. Add the chicken and turn to coat. Refrigerate for 3 or more hours, turning occasionally if possible.

Preheat the broiler to high and set an oven rack 3 to 4 inches from the heat. Lightly coat a foil-lined, rimmed baking sheet or broiler pan with nonstick cooking spray.

Remove the chicken from the marinade, letting any excess drip off, and place on the baking sheet. Broil the chicken for 4 to 6 minutes per side, or until just cooked through.

PER SERVING	
Calories	150
Calories from fat	25
Fat	3 g
Saturated fat	1 g
Trans fatty acids, total	0 g
Polyunsaturated fat	0.5 g
Monounsaturated fat	1 g
Cholesterol	65 mg
Sodium	310 mg
Carbohydrate	3 g
Dietary fiber	0 g
Sugars	2 g
Protein	27 g

 TIP *Generally, boneless chicken breasts are unevenly shaped. For more consistent cooking, gently pound the thicker part with a mallet to even them out.*

SHRIMP AND MULTICOLORED PEPPERS

This colorful, quick-cooking dish delivers a lot of flavor in less than fifteen minutes! A shower of orange zest and fresh basil at the end of cooking lends vibrancy with very little effort.

Cook the shrimp until just done, as it will continue to cook after being removed from the heat, especially when surrounded by hot vegetables. Overcooking seafood will cause it to become dry and rubbery and lose much of its flavor.

4 SERVINGS

1 tablespoon olive oil

1 onion, halved and thinly sliced

1 red bell pepper, seeded and cut into 1-inch pieces

1 yellow bell pepper, seeded and cut into 1-inch pieces

3 garlic cloves, minced

1 jalapeño pepper, seeded and finely chopped

1 (14.5-ounce) can diced tomatoes

1 pound large shrimp, peeled, deveined, and patted dry

2 tablespoons chopped fresh basil or 1 teaspoon dried

Zest of 1 orange

Salt and freshly ground black pepper

In a large, preferably nonstick, skillet over medium-high heat, add the oil. Sauté the onion and bell peppers for 5 to 8 minutes, or until softened. Add the garlic and jalapeño and sauté for 1 minute. Add the tomatoes and their juice and boil until the juices thicken, stirring to dislodge any bits of food that might have stuck to the bottom of the skillet. Reduce the heat to medium-low; add the shrimp, basil, and orange zest; and simmer for 2 to 4 minutes, or until the shrimp are just cooked through, stirring frequently. Season with salt and pepper.

PER SERVING

Calories	180
Calories from fat	45
Fat	5 g
Saturated fat	1 g
Trans fatty acids, total	0 g
Polyunsaturated fat	1 g
Monounsaturated fat	3 g
Cholesterol	150 mg
Sodium	480 mg
Carbohydrate	15 g
Dietary fiber	3 g
Sugars	7 g
Protein	19 g

If you don't have fresh basil on hand, you can use dried—just add it at the same time as the garlic instead of at the end of cooking. A pinch or two of cayenne pepper can be substituted for the jalapeño.

TURKEY-FETA BURGERS WITH YOGURT SAUCE

These burgers get a Greek twist with feta cheese, olives, and mint mixed into the turkey for dynamic flavoring. Topping them with a yogurt and cucumber sauce, known as tzatziki, provides the finishing touch. To give the sauce more zing, add olives, feta, mint, or if you have some on hand, fresh dill.

4 SERVINGS

SAUCE

1 cup nonfat plain Greek yogurt

1/2 cucumber, peeled, seeded, and chopped

1 garlic clove, minced

1 teaspoon fresh lemon juice

2 to 3 shakes hot sauce, or to taste

Salt and freshly ground black pepper

BURGERS

8 pitted kalamata olives, chopped

2 scallions, white and light green parts only, thinly sliced

1 garlic clove, minced

2 tablespoons chopped fresh mint

3 tablespoons nonfat plain Greek yogurt

1/2 cup crumbled feta cheese

1/2 teaspoon salt

1 pound ground turkey breast

1 tablespoon canola oil

FOR THE SAUCE: In a bowl, combine the yogurt, cucumber, garlic, lemon juice, and hot sauce. Season with salt, pepper, and additional hot sauce, if desired.

FOR THE BURGERS: In a bowl, combine the olives, scallions, garlic, and mint. Add the yogurt, feta, and salt and stir to combine. Add the turkey and stir gently to combine. Form into four patties.

In a large, preferably nonstick, skillet over medium heat, add the oil. Cook the burgers for 5 to 7 minutes per side, or until the turkey is cooked through and the tops and bottoms are golden brown and lightly crusted. If the burgers are very thick, cover the skillet for the last 3 minutes of cooking. Serve on whole wheat buns or pitas with a dollop of sauce.

PER SERVING

Calories	260
Calories from fat	90
Fat	10 g
Saturated fat	3.5 g
Trans fatty acids, total	0 g
Polyunsaturated fat	1.5 g
Monounsaturated fat	4 g
Cholesterol	90 mg
Sodium	640 mg
Carbohydrate	6 g
Dietary fiber	Less than 1 g
Sugars	4 g
Protein	37 g

HONEY-LIME PORK TENDERLOIN

In this delicious entrée, a coating of honey provides a sumptuous glaze, and a hint of lime balances that sweetness. Because pork is now raised to be much leaner, new recommendations suggest cooking it to only 145 to 150 degrees to keep the meat tender and moist. Don't be concerned if it is slightly pink in the center after slicing; it's safe to eat.

4 SERVINGS

4 garlic cloves, minced

2 limes, zested and juiced

2 tablespoons olive oil

2 tablespoons honey

Pinch crushed red pepper flakes

1 (1- to 1¼-pound) pork tenderloin

In a zip-top bag or bowl, combine the garlic, lime juice and zest, oil, honey, and red pepper flakes. Add the pork and turn to coat. Refrigerate for 3 or more hours, turning occasionally if possible.

Preheat the oven to 450 degrees.

Lightly coat a foil-lined, rimmed baking sheet with nonstick cooking spray.

Remove the pork from the marinade, letting any excess drip off. Reserve the marinade. Place the pork on the baking sheet and roast for 20 to 25 minutes, or until an instant-read thermometer registers 145 to 150 degrees, turning every 10 minutes. Let rest for 5 minutes before slicing.

Meanwhile, transfer the marinade to a saucepan and bring to a boil. Reduce the heat and simmer for 2 minutes, swirling the pan frequently. Drizzle the sliced pork with the sauce.

PER SERVING

Calories	220
Calories from fat	90
Fat	10 g
Saturated fat	2 g
Trans fatty acids, total	0 g
Polyunsaturated fat	1 g
Monounsaturated fat	6 g
Cholesterol	60 mg
Sodium	45 mg
Carbohydrate	11 g
Dietary fiber	0 g
Sugars	9 g
Protein	22 g

Start marinating the tenderloin in the morning so it's infused with flavor by the time you get home. Pork tenderloin can also be broiled or grilled. Use any leftover meat in a sandwich or salad for lunch.

FOUR-PEPPER CHICKEN CHILI

This colorful chili has four, count them, four types of peppers: poblano, bell, jalapeño, and chipotle (not to mention good old chili powder). This is an ideal dish to use up leftover roast chicken, although truthfully, there are enough veggies and beans to make the chicken optional!

If you are watching your sodium intake, choose no-salt-added beans and tomatoes and substitute homemade broth (page 206) for store-bought.

4 TO 6 SERVINGS

1 tablespoon canola oil

1 onion, chopped

1 poblano pepper, seeded and chopped

1 red, yellow, orange, or green bell pepper, seeded and chopped

1 jalapeño pepper, seeded and finely chopped

2 garlic cloves, minced

1 chipotle chile in adobo sauce, finely chopped

1 tablespoon ground cumin

1 tablespoon chili powder

1/2 teaspoon ground coriander

1/2 teaspoon dried oregano

2 (15-ounce) cans cannellini or navy beans, rinsed and drained, divided use

4 cups reduced-sodium chicken broth, divided use

1 (14.5-ounce) can diced tomatoes, drained

2 cups shredded cooked chicken breast

1 cup corn

Salt and freshly ground black pepper

1/4 cup chopped fresh cilantro

In a stockpot over medium heat, add the oil. Sauté the onion, poblano, bell pepper, and jalapeño for 5 to 8 minutes, or until softened. Add the garlic and chipotle and sauté for 1 minute. Add the cumin, chili powder, coriander, and oregano and stir to combine.

Meanwhile, in a food processor or blender, purée one can of the beans with 1 cup of the broth. Add to the stockpot with the remaining 3 cups of broth and tomatoes and bring to a boil, stirring to combine. Reduce the heat and simmer for 15 to 20 minutes, or until thickened, stirring occasionally. Add the chicken, corn, and the remaining can of beans and cook for 5 minutes. Season with salt and pepper and sprinkle with cilantro.

PER SERVING

Calories	400
Calories from fat	70
Fat	8 g
Saturated fat	1 g
Trans fatty acids, total	0 g
Polyunsaturated fat	2 g
Monounsaturated fat	3.5 g
Cholesterol	60 mg
Sodium	810 mg
Carbohydrate	48 g
Dietary fiber	12 g
Sugars	8 g
Protein	38 g

 Beans are an inexpensive and filling source of cholesterol-free protein. Low in fat and sodium, yet high in soluble and insoluble fiber, beans are a great source of complex carbohydrates and provide many valuable nutrients to vegetarian and vegan entrées.

SALMON BOWL WITH ASIAN DIPPING SAUCE

Steaming seafood is easier than you might think and has many benefits. It's easy, keeps the fish moist during cooking, and uses no fat. It's also fast, and in this dish, topping the fish with an assortment of vegetables makes for a complete meal in only minutes. Start the rice before you prep the veggies so it's ready when the salmon is finished cooking.

If you have extra time, make brown rice; begin it thirty minutes before the rest of the recipe.

2 SERVINGS

1/2 cup basmati or jasmine rice

2 (4- to 6-ounce) salmon fillets

1 cup small broccoli florets

1/2 cup snow peas, trimmed

1/2 cup snap peas, trimmed

1/4 cup sliced shiitake mushrooms

2 tablespoons reduced-sodium soy sauce

1 tablespoon rice vinegar

1 tablespoon mirin

1/2 teaspoon dark sesame oil

1 scallion, white and light green parts only, thinly sliced

Prepare the rice according to the package directions.

Meanwhile, lightly coat a steamer basket with nonstick cooking spray and place the salmon inside. Set the basket in a large saucepan filled with 1 to 2 inches of water (the water shouldn't reach the steamer). Place over medium-high heat, cover, and cook for 6 to 9 minutes, or until almost cooked through. Add the broccoli to the steamer and cook for 1 minute. Add the snow peas, snap peas, and mushrooms and cook for 1 minute, or until just cooked through.

In a bowl, combine the soy sauce, vinegar, mirin, and sesame oil and microwave on high for 30 seconds to warm. Add the scallion.

Divide the rice, salmon, and vegetables between two bowls. Drizzle with the sauce and serve remaining sauce on the side for dipping, if desired.

PER SERVING

Calories	380
Calories from fat	70
Fat	8 g
Saturated fat	1.5 g
Trans fatty acids, total	0 g
Polyunsaturated fat	3 g
Monounsaturated fat	2.5 g
Cholesterol	60 mg
Sodium	560 mg
Carbohydrate	41 g
Dietary fiber	3 g
Sugars	3 g
Protein	31 g

 Mirin is a type of sweetened rice wine, also sometimes labeled as sweetened sake. You should be able to find it in the international food aisle of your supermarket.

LEMON-ORANGE TILAPIA

Citrus is a wonderful complement to fish. In this elegant dish, tart fresh lemon juice and sweet orange juice combine for a winning pan sauce. Make this in the winter when the fruit is bursting with juices.

4 SERVINGS

2 tablespoons all-purpose flour

1/4 teaspoon salt

1/4 teaspoon freshly ground black pepper

4 (4- to 6-ounce) tilapia fillets

1 tablespoon olive oil

Juice of 2 oranges

Juice of 1 lemon

2 teaspoons honey

On a plate, combine the flour, salt, and pepper. Add the tilapia and coat with flour.

In a large skillet over medium-high heat, add the oil. Cook the tilapia for 2 to 3 minutes per side, or until just cooked through and golden brown. Remove the tilapia and set aside. Add the orange juice, lemon juice, and honey and boil until the sauce thickens, stirring to dislodge any bits of food that might have stuck to the bottom of the skillet. Reduce the heat to medium-low, return the tilapia to the skillet, and cook for 1 to 2 minutes, or until the tilapia is heated through and coated with sauce.

PER SERVING	
Calories	190
Calories from fat	50
Fat	6 g
Saturated fat	1.5 g
Trans fatty acids, total	0 g
Polyunsaturated fat	1 g
Monounsaturated fat	3.5 g
Cholesterol	50 mg
Sodium	200 mg
Carbohydrate	11 g
Dietary fiber	0 g
Sugars	7 g
Protein	23 g

 Seafood should never smell "fishy" or have an unpleasant or ammonia-like odor. Fish should look firm, moist, and translucent. Avoid slimy, dried-out, or discolored fish.

CHICKEN THIGHS WITH CHIPOTLE-TOMATO SAUCE

In this Mexican-inspired stew, a spicy chipotle-flavored tomato sauce and chicken thighs are cooked separately on the stovetop (no need to wash the pan in between) and then baked together. Serve over rice or another grain, or wrap the mixture in tortillas and top with a few chunks of avocado or chopped red onion. If serving with tortillas, wrap them in aluminum foil and bake at 350 degrees for ten minutes.

6 SERVINGS

1 tablespoon canola oil

1 onion, chopped

2 garlic cloves, minced

$1/2$ teaspoon dried oregano

1 (14.5-ounce) can diced tomatoes

1 to 2 chipotle chiles in adobo sauce, finely chopped

$1/2$ cup reduced-sodium chicken broth

Salt and freshly ground black pepper

$1 1/2$ pounds boneless, skinless chicken thighs, trimmed of excess fat

Tortillas or rice, optional

Preheat the oven to 350 degrees.

In a large skillet over medium-high heat, add the oil. Sauté the onion for 3 to 5 minutes, or until softened. Add the garlic and oregano and sauté for 1 minute. Add the tomatoes and their juice, 1 chipotle, and broth and bring to a boil. Reduce the heat and simmer for 20 minutes, or until thickened, stirring occasionally. Season with salt and pepper and additional chipotle, if desired. Transfer to a blender or food processor and let cool slightly before puréeing until smooth.

Meanwhile, sprinkle the chicken with salt and pepper. In the same skillet, over medium-high heat, cook the chicken for 3 to 4 minutes per side. It will not be cooked through.

Transfer the chicken to a 9- or 8-inch baking pan and top with the puréed tomato sauce. Bake for 45 to 50 minutes, or until the chicken is tender and

the sauce has thickened. Remove the chicken to a cutting board, reserving the sauce. When cool enough to handle, use your fingers or two forks to shred into small pieces. Return the chicken to the sauce and stir to combine. Serve with tortillas or rice, if desired.

PER SERVING

Calories	180
Calories from fat	80
Fat	9 g
Saturated fat	2 g
Trans fatty acids, total	0 g
Polyunsaturated fat	2 g
Monounsaturated fat	4 g
Cholesterol	105 mg
Sodium	220 mg
Carbohydrate	6 g
Dietary fiber	1 g
Sugars	3 g
Protein	19 g

TIP *Taste the sauce during cooking—one chipotle should provide enough heat, but if you really like it spicy, add another half or a whole pepper.*

FLANK STEAK BURRITO BOWLS WITH CORN SALSA

Why go to a fast food place for a burrito bowl when you can make a healthier one at home for less? Brown rice mixed with fresh cilantro forms the base for grilled flank steak, black beans, and a tangy corn salsa. Chopped romaine lettuce, avocado, grated cheese, and a lime wedge complete this "one bowl" meal.

4 SERVINGS

1 cup brown rice

1 pound flank, hanger, or skirt steak, trimmed of excess fat

2 tablespoons "Mexican" or "Southwest" seasoning blend

Salt and freshly ground black pepper

2 cups cooked corn

2 tablespoons finely chopped poblano or bell pepper

2 tablespoons finely chopped red onion

1 tablespoon finely chopped jalapeño pepper

1 tomato, seeded and chopped

1 lime, cut into six wedges, divided use

1 teaspoon extra-virgin olive oil

1/2 cup chopped fresh cilantro

1 (15-ounce) can black beans, rinsed, drained, and heated

1 avocado, cut into 1/2-inch pieces

1 cup chopped romaine lettuce

1/2 cup shredded Cheddar or Mexican-blend cheese

Salsa, optional

Prepare the rice according to the package directions.

Preheat a grill pan over medium-high heat for 1 minute and lightly coat with nonstick cooking spray.

Coat the steak with the seasoning blend. Season with salt and pepper. Cook the steak for 4 to 6 minutes per side for medium-rare. Let rest for 5 minutes before slicing on the diagonal, against the grain, into thin strips. Cut the strips into bite-sized pieces.

Meanwhile, in a bowl, combine the corn, poblano, onion, jalapeño, and tomato. Squeeze two pieces of lime over the mixture, drizzle with the oil, and stir to combine. Season with salt and pepper.

Add the cilantro to the rice. Divide the rice between four bowls. Top each bowl with meat, corn salad, black beans, and a wedge of lime. Sprinkle with the avocado, lettuce, and cheese. Serve with salsa, if desired.

PER SERVING

Calories	590
Calories from fat	160
Fat	18 g
Saturated fat	6 g
Trans fatty acids, total	0 g
Polyunsaturated fat	2 g
Monounsaturated fat	9 g
Cholesterol	70 mg
Sodium	210 mg
Carbohydrate	72 g
Dietary fiber	14 g
Sugars	6 g
Protein	38 g

 This dish can also be made with chicken, pork tenderloin, or tofu.

SWEET AND SOUR CHICKEN WITH PINEAPPLE

Instead of ordering Chinese takeout, prepare this delicious dish at home. Don't worry if the chicken sticks to the pan while it's browning. That residual crust will add flavor that's incorporated when you deglaze the pan.

When buying fresh precut pineapple, there's usually two to four tablespoons of juice in the container. If cutting your own pineapple, slice it over a bowl to catch all the liquid.

4 SERVINGS

1 pound boneless, skinless chicken breasts, cut into 1-inch pieces

1 tablespoon cornstarch

1 tablespoon canola oil

1 onion, cut into 1-inch pieces

1 red bell pepper, seeded and cut into 1-inch pieces

1 celery stalk, cut into 1-inch pieces

1 1/2 cups fresh pineapple, cut into 1-inch pieces, juices reserved, divided use

2 garlic cloves, minced

1 teaspoon minced fresh ginger

1/4 teaspoon crushed red pepper flakes

1/4 cup light brown sugar

1/4 cup white vinegar

1/4 cup ketchup

1 tablespoon reduced-sodium soy sauce

Pat chicken dry and place in a bowl. Add the cornstarch and stir to coat.

In a large skillet over medium heat, add the oil. Cook the chicken for 2 to 3 minutes per side, or until just cooked through. Remove the chicken and set aside. Add the onion, bell pepper, and celery and sauté for 3 to 5 minutes, or until softened. Add the pineapple, garlic, ginger, and red pepper flakes and sauté for 1 minute.

Meanwhile, in a bowl, combine the reserved pineapple juice, brown sugar, vinegar, ketchup, and soy sauce. Add to the skillet and simmer, stirring to dislodge any bits of food that might have stuck to the bottom of the skillet. Reduce the heat to medium-low, return the chicken and any accumulated juices to the skillet, and cook for 1 to 2 minutes, or until the chicken is heated through and coated with sauce.

PER SERVING	
Calories	290
Calories from fat	60
Fat	7 g
Saturated fat	1 g
Trans fatty acids, total	0 g
Polyunsaturated fat	1.5 g
Monounsaturated fat	3 g
Cholesterol	65 mg
Sodium	380 mg
Carbohydrate	31 g
Dietary fiber	3 g
Sugars	23 g
Protein	26 g

 Poultry is a nutritional winner. Not only low in fat and calories, it's a good source of vitamins B2, B6, B12, riboflavin, niacin, zinc, and magnesium.

CHICKEN PAILLARD WITH ARUGULA AND FENNEL

In this dish, thin chicken cutlets are flash-cooked and topped with an enticing mixture of arugula and fennel for a light, fresh-tasting dinner.

A paillard is a piece of chicken or meat pounded until it is very thin and almost doubled in size and then cooked quickly. If you don't have the patience to pound properly, there are several tricks you can use to speed up the process. One is to butterfly each breast by cutting partially through it so it opens like a book, creating one very large piece to pound. Other ways are to buy "thin-sliced" boneless chicken cutlets, or to make your own by slicing each breast in half lengthwise and then using a mallet to compress those slices. These methods will give you pieces about half of the size of using a full breast so you might need two pieces per serving.

Use a mandoline or a very sharp knife to thinly slice the fennel.

4 SERVINGS

4 cups arugula

1 fennel bulb, halved, thick core and fronds removed, very thinly sliced

1 tablespoon extra-virgin olive oil

1 to 2 tablespoons fresh lemon juice

Salt and freshly ground black pepper

1 pound boneless, skinless chicken breasts

1 tablespoon olive oil

1 cup shaved Parmesan cheese

In a bowl, combine the arugula and fennel. Drizzle with the extra-virgin olive oil and stir gently to combine. Drizzle with 1 tablespoon lemon juice and stir gently to combine. Season with salt and pepper and additional lemon juice, if desired.

With a mallet, pound the chicken breasts between wax paper until they are between 1/4- and 1/2-inch thick. Sprinkle the chicken with salt and pepper.

In a large skillet over medium-high heat, add the olive oil. Cook the chicken for 2 to 3 minutes per side, or until just cooked through and golden brown. You will probably be able to fit only two pieces of chicken in the skillet at a time. Remove the chicken and tent with aluminum foil to keep warm. Repeat with the other pieces.

Top the chicken with the salad and Parmesan shavings.

PER SERVING

Calories	250
Calories from fat	110
Fat	12 g
Saturated fat	3.5 g
Trans fatty acids, total	0 g
Polyunsaturated fat	1.5 g
Monounsaturated fat	7 g
Cholesterol	75 mg
Sodium	240 mg
Carbohydrate	4 g
Dietary fiber	2 g
Sugars	2 g
Protein	29 g

TIP *When making a salad, experiment with different greens, such as peppery arugula and buttery baby lettuce. Other bitter leaf vegetables such as crisp endive and radicchio add unique flavors. Fennel has a licorice-like flavor and adds crunch.*

MAPLE-MUSTARD SALMON

Even non–fish eaters will dig into this delicious dish, with its balance of sweet and spicy (with two types of mustard no less)! Look for whole grain mustard with visible mustard seeds in the condiment aisle.

A silicone brush is perfect for spreading the sauce on the salmon.

4 SERVINGS

2 tablespoons whole grain mustard

1 tablespoon pure maple syrup

1 teaspoon Dijon mustard

1/2 teaspoon ground ginger

4 (4- to 6-ounce) salmon fillets

Salt and freshly ground black pepper

Preheat the oven to 450 degrees.

Lightly coat a foil-lined, rimmed baking sheet with nonstick cooking spray.

In a bowl, combine the whole grain mustard, maple syrup, Dijon mustard, and ginger. Place the salmon, skin side down, on the baking sheet. Brush lightly with the sauce and sprinkle with salt and pepper. Bake for 10 minutes. Remove and top with the remaining sauce. Bake for 3 to 8 minutes, or until the fish is cooked through.

PER SERVING	
Calories	200
Calories from fat	70
Fat	8 g
Saturated fat	2 g
Trans fatty acids, total	0 g
Polyunsaturated fat	2 g
Monounsaturated fat	3 g
Cholesterol	65 mg
Sodium	210 mg
Carbohydrate	4 g
Dietary fiber	0 g
Sugars	3 g
Protein	23 g

 TIP *The cooking time will vary according to the thickness of your salmon fillets. Try to get similarly sized pieces (or cut a large piece into four equally sized fillets). If there are pieces of varying size, let the thicker pieces cook for an extra few minutes.*

TURKEY CUTLETS WITH ORANGE-CRANBERRY GLAZE

The flavors of turkey and cranberries needn't be relegated to only one day a year. Many supermarkets now sell boneless, skinless turkey cutlets or boneless turkey breasts all year round, making them an easy choice for an unexpected everyday dinner. If you can't find sliced cutlets, look for turkey "London broil" or tenderloin and cut into $^1/_2$-inch thick slices.

Use a food processor to chop the cranberries quickly.

4 SERVINGS

$^1/_4$ cup all-purpose flour

$^1/_4$ teaspoon salt

$^1/_4$ teaspoon freshly ground black pepper

1 pound turkey breast cutlets, pounded or sliced to even thickness

2 tablespoons canola oil, divided use

$^1/_4$ cup chopped red onion

1 garlic clove, minced

1 cup fresh orange juice

$^3/_4$ cup fresh cranberries, coarsely chopped

2 tablespoons light brown sugar

1 tablespoon balsamic vinegar

On a plate, combine the flour, salt, and pepper. Add the turkey and coat with flour.

In a large skillet over medium-high heat, add 1 tablespoon of the oil. Cook the turkey for 3 to 4 minutes per side, or until just cooked through and golden brown. Remove the turkey and set aside. Add the remaining 1 tablespoon of oil and sauté the onion for 2 to 3 minutes. Add the garlic and sauté for 1 minute. Add the orange juice, cranberries, brown sugar, and vinegar and boil until the sauce has thickened and reduced by half, stirring to dislodge any bits of food that have stuck to the bottom of the skillet. Reduce the heat to medium-low, return the turkey and any accumulated juices to the skillet, and cook for 1 to 2 minutes, or until the turkey is heated through and coated with sauce.

PER SERVING	
Calories	240
Calories from fat	70
Fat	8 g
Saturated fat	0.5 g
Trans fatty acids, total	0 g
Polyunsaturated fat	2 g
Monounsaturated fat	4.5 g
Cholesterol	55 mg
Sodium	110 mg
Carbohydrate	20 g
Dietary fiber	1 g
Sugars	14 g
Protein	21 g

Keep a bag of cranberries in your freezer to use year-round in recipes like this and the Cranberry, Orange, and Ginger Compote on page 161.

CRISPY TOFU WITH LEMONGRASS AND PEPPERS

This is the dish to convert even the most ardent tofu-resisters. The combination of fish sauce, lemongrass, and honey creates a delicious balance of salty and sweet.

If you are watching your sodium intake, start with two tablespoons of fish sauce and add more to taste if needed. If you can't find chili paste (sambal oelek), substitute chili garlic sauce or Sriracha.

4 SERVINGS

1 (16-ounce) block extra-firm tofu

3 tablespoons cornstarch

2 tablespoons canola oil

4 garlic cloves, minced

2 fresh lemongrass stalks, tender part only, finely chopped

1 red onion, cut into 1-inch pieces

1 jalapeño pepper, seeded and finely chopped

1 red bell pepper, seeded and cut into 1-inch pieces

3 tablespoons fish sauce

1 tablespoon honey

1 teaspoon chili paste (sambal oelek)

Line a plate with paper towels and place the tofu on top. Cover with paper towels and top with another plate weighed down with cans or a heavy pot for 30 minutes to release excess water. Cut into 1-inch cubes and place in a bowl. Add the cornstarch and stir to coat.

In a large, preferably nonstick, skillet over medium-high heat, add the oil. Cook the tofu for 1 to 2 minutes per side, or until golden brown. Remove the tofu and set aside. Add the garlic, lemongrass, onion, jalapeño, and bell pepper and sauté for 5 to 8 minutes, or until softened.

Meanwhile, in a bowl, combine the fish sauce, honey, and chili paste. Add to the skillet. Reduce the heat to medium-low, return the tofu to the skillet, and cook for 1 to 2 minutes, or until the tofu is heated through and coated with sauce.

PER SERVING	
Calories	250
Calories from fat	110
Fat	12 g
Saturated fat	1 g
Trans fatty acids, total	0 g
Polyunsaturated fat	5 g
Monounsaturated fat	6 g
Cholesterol	0 mg
Sodium	1060 mg
Carbohydrate	24 g
Dietary fiber	3 g
Sugars	9 g
Protein	12 g

 Fish sauce is a mainstay in Thai cooking and is most often made from anchovies, salt, and water.

POACHED SHRIMP WITH MINT DRESSING

An easy way to add a lot of flavor without a lot of effort is to coat poached shrimp in a minty dressing after cooking, so the flavors are super vibrant. If you have parsley on hand, add a few tablespoons of that, as well.

4 SERVINGS

1 lemon, halved

1 pound shrimp, peeled, deveined, and patted dry

1 garlic clove

1 cup fresh mint

3 tablespoons extra-virgin olive oil

Salt and freshly ground black pepper

Squeeze 2 tablespoons juice from the lemon and reserve. Fill a saucepan with three inches of water. Thinly slice the remaining lemon (including the portion that was squeezed) and add to the saucepan. Bring to a boil. Reduce the heat to a low simmer. Add the shrimp and stir. Cook for 1 to 2 minutes, or until opaque and just cooked through. Drain, discard the lemon slices, and pat the shrimp dry.

Meanwhile, in a food processor with the motor running, add the garlic and mint. Scrape down the sides, add the oil and reserved lemon juice, and pulse to combine.

In a bowl, combine the shrimp and mint mixture. Season with salt and pepper.

PER SERVING

Calories	190
Calories from fat	100
Fat	12 g
Saturated fat	2 g
Trans fatty acids, total	0 g
Polyunsaturated fat	1.5 g
Monounsaturated fat	8 g
Cholesterol	150 mg
Sodium	340 mg
Carbohydrate	4 g
Dietary fiber	1 g
Sugars	Less than 1 g
Protein	17 g

For a more substantial meal, add the shrimp to the Farro Salad with Feta and Fresh Herbs (page 98) or the Quinoa Salad with Cranberries and Mint (page 120). The shrimp are also delicious on top of rice, pasta, salad, or even tucked into a sandwich.

EGGPLANT PARMESAN LIGHT

This healthier version of eggplant parmesan maintains the essence of the dish, but trades fried eggplant slices for baked ones and trims the amount of cheese used.

Because the eggplant is salted and cooked before it's combined with the other ingredients, allow an hour and a half to make this dish. Most of that time is hands-off, but the overall prep is longer than other recipes in this book.

8 SERVINGS

2 pounds eggplant, cut into 1/4-inch-thick rounds

1 teaspoon salt

4 egg whites

1/4 cup water

1 1/2 cups plain or seasoned bread crumbs

1 tablespoon olive oil

3 garlic cloves, minced

1 (28-ounce) can crushed tomatoes

1 teaspoon dried basil

1 teaspoon dried oregano

1 cup shredded part-skim mozzarella cheese

1/2 cup freshly grated Parmesan cheese

In a large colander, sprinkle the eggplant with salt and set in the sink to drain for 30 minutes.

Preheat the oven to 425 degrees. Place two large, foil-lined rimmed baking sheets in the oven to preheat.

When the eggplant is ready, place on a paper towel–lined plate or cutting board and press down with additional paper towels to absorb any excess moisture and salt. Remove the baking sheets from the oven and coat with nonstick cooking spray.

In a shallow bowl, beat the egg whites and water. Place the bread crumbs on a plate. Dip each eggplant slice into the egg mixture, letting any excess drip off, and coat with the bread crumbs, pressing to adhere. Place the slices in a single layer on the baking sheets and lightly coat them with nonstick cooking spray. Bake for 25 to 30 minutes, or until golden and tender, flipping the slices after 15 minutes. Remove the baking sheets from the oven and lower the heat to 400 degrees.

Meanwhile, in a large skillet over medium-high heat, add the oil. Sauté the garlic for 1 minute. Add the tomatoes, basil, and oregano and bring to a boil. Reduce the heat and simmer for 15 to 20 minutes, or until thickened, stirring occasionally.

In the bottom of a 9-by-13-inch baking dish, spread 1/2 cup of the sauce. Arrange half of the eggplant slices over the sauce, overlapping them slightly. Spoon half of the remaining sauce over the eggplant and top with half of the mozzarella and half of the Parmesan. Arrange the remaining eggplant slices in another layer. Top with the remaining sauce, mozzarella, and Parmesan. Bake for 15 to 20 minutes, or until the cheese melts. Let rest for 5 minutes before serving.

PER SERVING

Calories	210
Calories from fat	60
Fat	7 g
Saturated fat	2.5 g
Trans fatty acids, total	0 g
Polyunsaturated fat	1 g
Monounsaturated fat	2.5 g
Cholesterol	10 mg
Sodium	540 mg
Carbohydrate	30 g
Dietary fiber	5 g
Sugars	9 g
Protein	12 g

TIP *If you don't have time to make your own sauce, use your favorite jarred marinara.*

TORTELLINI WITH RED PEPPER SAUCE

Diners will be pleasantly surprised by this unexpected "red sauce." Don't worry about chopping the vegetables precisely because the sauce is puréed before serving. You just want similarly sized pieces for even cooking.

Be careful when puréeing hot liquids in a blender or food processor because the steam can create increased pressure. Let the sauce cool slightly before blending, and don't overfill the blender.

4 TO 6 SERVINGS

1 tablespoon olive oil

3 medium red bell peppers, seeded and chopped

1 onion, chopped

3 garlic cloves, minced

1/4 teaspoon crushed red pepper flakes, or to taste

1 cup reduced-sodium chicken or vegetable broth

1 tablespoon fresh lemon juice, or to taste

1 tablespoon fresh orange juice, or to taste

Salt and freshly ground black pepper

1 pound tortellini, ravioli, or other pasta

1/4 cup chopped fresh basil

In a large skillet over medium heat, add the oil. Sauté the bell peppers and onion for 8 to 10 minutes, or until softened. Add the garlic and red pepper flakes and sauté for 1 minute. Add the broth and bring to a boil. Reduce the heat, cover, and simmer for 15 to 20 minutes, or until the peppers are very tender, stirring occasionally. Transfer to a blender or food processor and let cool slightly before puréeing until smooth. Add the lemon and orange juices. Season with salt and pepper and additional lemon or orange juice and red pepper flakes, if desired.

Meanwhile, prepare the tortellini according to the package directions.

Place the tortellini in a bowl, add the sauce, and stir to combine. Top with the basil.

PER SERVING

Calories	390
Calories from fat	50
Fat	5 g
Saturated fat	0.5 g
Trans fatty acids, total	0 g
Polyunsaturated fat	1 g
Monounsaturated fat	2.5 g
Cholesterol	0 mg
Sodium	140 mg
Carbohydrate	71 g
Dietary fiber	6 g
Sugars	8 g
Protein	12 g

 Red bell peppers aren't just more visually appealing than standard green peppers, they also have a milder flavor and significantly more vitamins A and C.

CHIPOTLE TURKEY-BEAN TACOS

A fast food favorite gets a "good-for-you" makeover with ground turkey breast stepping in for beef. Instead of cheese or sour cream, the tacos are topped with avocado, which feels indulgent but has monounsaturated heart-healthy benefits.

If you are watching your sodium intake, choose no-salt-added beans and tomato sauce.

8 SERVINGS

1 tablespoon canola oil

1 small onion, finely chopped

1/2 green bell pepper, seeded and finely chopped

1 pound ground turkey breast

2 garlic cloves, minced

1 tablespoon chili powder

1 teaspoon ground cumin

1 (8-ounce) can tomato sauce

1 chipotle chile in adobo sauce, finely chopped

1 cup black beans, rinsed and drained

8 (5- to 6-inch) whole wheat, flour, or corn tortillas

1 avocado

1 tablespoon fresh lemon juice

Salt and freshly ground black pepper

Preheat the oven to 350 degrees.

In a large skillet over medium-high heat, add the oil. Sauté the onion and bell pepper for 3 to 5 minutes, or until softened. Add the turkey and sauté for 5 to 8 minutes, or until the turkey is cooked through and any excess liquid has evaporated. Add the garlic, chili powder, and cumin and sauté for 1 minute. Add the tomato sauce and chipotle, reduce the heat, and simmer, stirring to combine. Cook for 5 minutes, stirring occasionally. Add the beans and cook for 2 to 3 minutes, or until heated through. Season with salt and pepper.

Meanwhile, wrap the tortillas in aluminum foil and bake for 10 minutes. (Tortillas can also be wrapped in a damp towel and warmed in the microwave on high for 15 to 30 seconds.)

In a bowl, coarsely mash the avocado and stir gently with lemon juice. Season with salt.

Spoon the turkey mixture onto the tortillas and top with a dollop of avocado.

PER SERVING

Calories	245
Calories from fat	80
Fat	8 g
Saturated fat	2 g
Trans fatty acids, total	0 g
Polyunsaturated fat	2 g
Monounsaturated fat	4 g
Cholesterol	32 mg
Sodium	360 mg
Carbohydrate	23 g
Dietary fiber	7 g
Sugars	3 g
Protein	20 g

TIP *Canned chipotles add flavor to any taco dish. If you like things really hot, use another half or whole chipotle or more adobo sauce. For those who prefer milder flavors, start with half a chipotle and build from there. Since you usually only need one or two peppers at a time, freeze the rest individually with a little of the sauce in ice cube trays or plastic wrap. Once frozen, store in a zip-top bag for later use.*

SPINACH AND MUSHROOM RISOTTO

The secret to perfect risotto, a creamy rice dish made with short-grain, highly glutinous rice, is the gradual incorporation of liquid. Restaurant versions of risotto can be loaded with butter and heavy cream. This version still tastes rich, but has very little fat.

Before serving, drizzle individual portions with truffle oil, which is available at gourmet and many home-goods stores, or extra-virgin olive oil for a decadent touch.

4 SERVINGS

4 cups reduced-sodium chicken or vegetable broth

2 tablespoons olive oil, divided use

1/2 onion, finely chopped

1 garlic clove, minced

1 cup arborio or carnaroli "risotto" rice

1/2 cup dry white wine (such as sauvignon blanc or pinot grigio)

12 ounces assorted mushrooms (such as shiitake, cremini, and button), sliced

3 cups fresh baby spinach, coarsely chopped

1 teaspoon fresh thyme leaves

1/4 cup freshly grated Parmesan cheese

Salt and freshly ground black pepper

Truffle oil, optional

In a saucepan, bring the broth to a simmer. Cover and keep warm over low heat (you can also microwave the broth).

In a large stockpot over medium heat, add 1 tablespoon of the oil. Sauté the onion for 2 to 3 minutes. Add the garlic and sauté for 1 minute. Add the rice and sauté for 1 minute. Add the wine and stir until it is almost completely absorbed.

Begin slowly adding the broth, 1/2 cup at a time, stirring frequently. Wait until the liquid is almost completely absorbed before adding more, 2 to 4 minutes. Continue to add the broth, stirring frequently, for 20 to 30 minutes, or until the risotto has a creamy texture but is still al dente (just firm). You may not need to use all of the broth.

Meanwhile, in a skillet over medium-high heat, add the remaining 1 tablespoon of oil. Sauté the

mushrooms for 3 to 5 minutes, or until they have softened and released their liquid.

When the risotto is ready, stir in the spinach until wilted. Add the mushrooms, thyme, and cheese and stir to combine. Season with salt and pepper and serve immediately. Drizzle individual servings with truffle oil, if desired.

PER SERVING	
Calories	270
Calories from fat	70
Fat	7 g
Saturated fat	1 g
Trans fatty acids, total	0 g
Polyunsaturated fat	1 g
Monounsaturated fat	5 g
Cholesterol	0 mg
Sodium	540 mg
Carbohydrate	40 g
Dietary fiber	2 g
Sugars	3 g
Protein	9 g

TIP *When a recipe calls for wine, choose a wine that you would drink on its own. It needn't be expensive, but it must be drinkable. If you wish to cook without alcohol, replace with additional broth.*

CORNMEAL-CRUSTED FISH "FRY" WITH CAPER SAUCE

Instead of the typical oil-laden fried fish, these baked cornmeal-coated fish fillets still come out crispy, but with less fat and mess. If you need to take this meal to go, put fillets on whole wheat rolls with lettuce and tomato slices and top with the caper sauce and Honey Coleslaw (page 146), or serve the slaw on the side, if you prefer.

4 SERVINGS

FISH

1 egg

1 tablespoon Dijon mustard

3/4 cup yellow cornmeal

1/2 teaspoon dried thyme

1/4 teaspoon cayenne pepper

4 (4- to 6-ounce) tilapia or other white fish fillets

SAUCE

1/3 cup "light" or reduced-fat mayonnaise

1 tablespoon Dijon mustard

1 tablespoon chopped cornichons or other pickles

1 tablespoon chopped capers

2 teaspoons fresh lemon juice

2 to 3 shakes hot sauce, or to taste

Salt

FOR THE FISH: Preheat the oven to 425 degrees. Lightly coat a foil-lined, rimmed baking sheet with nonstick cooking spray.

In a shallow bowl, beat the egg and mustard. On a plate, combine the cornmeal, thyme, and cayenne pepper. Dip each fillet into the egg mixture, letting any excess drip off, and coat with the cornmeal mixture, pressing to adhere.

Place the fish fillets on the baking sheet and lightly coat them with nonstick cooking spray. Bake for 8 to 12 minutes, or until just cooked through, flipping the fish after 5 minutes.

FOR THE SAUCE: Meanwhile, in a bowl, combine the mayonnaise, mustard, cornichons, capers, lemon juice, and hot sauce. Season with salt and additional hot sauce, if desired.

Top each fillet with a dollop of caper sauce.

PER SERVING

Calories	270
Calories from fat	80
Fat	9 g
Saturated fat	2 g
Trans fatty acids, total	0 g
Polyunsaturated fat	3.5 g
Monounsaturated fat	3 g
Cholesterol	100 mg
Sodium	430 mg
Carbohydrate	21 g
Dietary fiber	1 g
Sugars	2 g
Protein	26 g

SALMON TERIYAKI

This seafood dish will please even the pickiest eaters. Making your own teriyaki sauce takes only minutes and ensures you aren't getting a lot of sugar and additives.

The baking time will vary according to the thickness of your salmon fillets. Try to get similarly sized pieces (or cut a large piece into equal sizes). For easier cleanup, line your baking pan with aluminum foil. Serve with brown rice and steamed broccoli.

4 SERVINGS

1/4 cup reduced-sodium soy sauce

2 tablespoons honey

2 tablespoons water

1 teaspoon minced fresh ginger

1 garlic clove, minced

2 scallions, white and light green parts only, thinly sliced

4 (4- to 6-ounce) salmon fillets

1 teaspoon sesame seeds, optional

Preheat the oven to 450 degrees.

In a small saucepan over medium-low heat, bring the soy sauce, honey, water, ginger, and garlic to a simmer. Transfer to a bowl, add the scallions, and stir to combine. Set aside to cool briefly.

Place the salmon skin side down in a baking pan. Pour the sauce over the fish and bake for 13 to 18 minutes, or until just cooked through, basting every 5 minutes. Sprinkle with sesame seeds, if desired.

PER SERVING	
Calories	220
Calories from fat	70
Fat	8 g
Saturated fat	2 g
Trans fatty acids, total	0 g
Polyunsaturated fat	2 g
Monounsaturated fat	3 g
Cholesterol	65 mg
Sodium	630 mg
Carbohydrate	11 g
Dietary fiber	0 g
Sugars	9 g
Protein	25 g

 TIP *Optional ingredients, such as the sesame seeds used in this recipe, enhance the presentation and the flavor. But if you don't have them, don't let it stop you from making the dish! It's still delicious without.*

PENNE WITH BROCCOLI RABE AND WHITE BEANS

When cooking with whole wheat pasta, you need stronger flavors that won't be overwhelmed by its assertiveness. In this recipe, broccoli rabe adds a bit of bitterness, which is mellowed by the creamy cannellini beans. For more cheese flavor, grate your own Parmesan cheese.

4 SERVINGS

8 ounces whole wheat penne or other shaped pasta

1 pound broccoli rabe, heavy stems removed, cut into 1- to 2-inch pieces

2 tablespoons olive oil

10 garlic cloves, thinly sliced

1/2 teaspoon crushed red pepper flakes, or to taste

2 cups reduced-sodium chicken or vegetable broth

2 (15-ounce) cans cannellini beans, rinsed and drained

1 tablespoon extra-virgin olive oil

1/4 cup freshly grated Parmesan cheese

Salt and freshly ground black pepper

Prepare the penne according to the package directions for al dente (just firm). About 2 minutes before the pasta is ready, add the broccoli rabe. Reserve 1/4 cup of the pasta water before draining.

Meanwhile, in a large skillet over medium heat, add the olive oil. Sauté the garlic and red pepper flakes for 1 minute. Add the broth and boil for 3 to 5 minutes, or until reduced by half, stirring frequently. Reduce the heat to medium, add the beans, and cook for 2 to 3 minutes, or until heated through. Add the pasta and broccoli rabe and stir until coated with sauce. Transfer to a bowl. Drizzle with the extra-virgin olive oil (if dry, also add a tablespoon or so of reserved cooking liquid). Top with the cheese and season generously with salt and pepper and additional red pepper flakes, if desired.

PER SERVING

Calories	520
Calories from fat	120
Fat	14 g
Saturated fat	2 g
Trans fatty acids, total	0 g
Polyunsaturated fat	2 g
Monounsaturated fat	8 g
Cholesterol	Less than 5 mg
Sodium	500 mg
Carbohydrate	79 g
Dietary fiber	17 g
Sugars	3 g
Protein	24 g

 TIP *Freshly grating a block of Parmesan cheese (try Parmigiano-Reggiano for authenticity) saves calories and fat. Besides having superior flavor, freshly grated cheese is so much lighter; it weighs half as much as the equivalent amount of packaged grated cheese. Try using a Microplane, a sharp, handheld grater.*

CURRIED VEGETABLES

The more veggies, the better in this one-pot vegetarian dish flavored with curry powder and other aromatic spices. Use whatever produce you have on hand—you really can't go wrong. Add longer-cooking vegetables earlier in the recipe (or cut them into smaller pieces) so that everything ends up evenly cooked.

6 SERVINGS

2 tablespoons canola oil

1 onion, chopped

1 tablespoon curry powder

1 teaspoon garam masala

1 teaspoon ground cumin

1/2 teaspoon ground turmeric

1/4 teaspoon ground cinnamon

1/4 teaspoon crushed red pepper flakes, or to taste

1 sweet potato, peeled and cut into 3/4-inch pieces

1/2 head cauliflower, cored and cut into florets

1 red bell pepper, seeded and cut into 3/4-inch pieces

1 cup reduced-sodium chicken or vegetable broth

1 (14.5-ounce) can fire-roasted or plain diced tomatoes

1 (15-ounce) can chickpeas, rinsed and drained

1 (5- or 6-ounce) package fresh baby spinach

Salt and freshly ground black pepper

In a stockpot over medium heat, add the oil. Sauté the onion for 3 to 5 minutes, or until softened. Add the curry powder, garam masala, cumin, turmeric, cinnamon, and red pepper flakes and stir to combine. Add the sweet potato and sauté for 3 minutes. Add the cauliflower and bell pepper and sauté for 2 minutes. Add the broth and the tomatoes and their juice and bring to a boil. Reduce the heat, cover, and simmer for 15 minutes, stirring occasionally. Add the chickpeas and cook for 2 minutes. Add the spinach and stir to combine. Let rest for 2 to 3 minutes before serving, stirring occasionally. Season with salt and pepper and additional red pepper flakes, if desired.

PER SERVING

Calories	200
Calories from fat	60
Fat	6.5 g
Saturated fat	0.5 g
Trans fatty acids, total	0 g
Polyunsaturated fat	2 g
Monounsaturated fat	3.5 g
Cholesterol	0 mg
Sodium	370 mg
Carbohydrate	29 g
Dietary fiber	8 g
Sugars	9 g
Protein	7 g

To lessen the intensity of the seasonings, cut back on the spices or top the stew with a dollop of Greek yogurt or a sprinkling of golden raisins. Serve over brown rice, barley, or quinoa for a complete meal.

MARINATED FLANK STEAK WITH THAI SLAW

The best way to incorporate red meat into a meal is in a supporting role. This spicy beef and slaw recipe balances a higher-fat protein with lots of fiber-filled veggies. If you are watching your sodium intake, start with one tablespoon of fish sauce in the slaw and add more to taste.

4 SERVINGS

STEAK

2 tablespoons fish sauce

Juice of 1 lime

1 tablespoon reduced-sodium soy sauce

3 garlic cloves, chopped

1 jalapeño pepper, seeded and chopped

1 pound flank, hanger, or skirt steak, trimmed of excess fat

SLAW

$1/2$ head white cabbage, thinly sliced or shredded

2 carrots, shredded

1 bunch fresh cilantro, chopped, about $1/2$ to 1 cup

1 bunch fresh mint, chopped, about $1/2$ to 1 cup

2 shallots or $1/2$ red onion, thinly sliced

1 small jalapeño pepper, seeded and chopped

2 tablespoons fish sauce

2 tablespoons fresh lime juice

2 to 3 tablespoons granulated sugar

FOR THE STEAK: In a zip-top bag or bowl, combine the fish sauce, lime juice, soy sauce, garlic, and jalapeño. Add the steak and turn to coat. Refrigerate for 3 or more hours, turning occasionally if possible.

FOR THE SLAW: In a bowl, combine the cabbage, carrots, cilantro, mint, shallots, and jalapeño. In a separate bowl, combine the fish sauce, lime juice, and 2 tablespoons of the sugar. Add more sugar, if desired. Add to the slaw and stir well to combine.

Preheat the broiler to high and set an oven rack 3 to 4 inches from the heat. Lightly coat a foil-lined, rimmed baking sheet or broiler pan with nonstick cooking spray.

Remove the steak from the marinade, letting excess drip off, and place on the baking sheet. Broil the steak for 4 to 6 minutes per side for medium-rare. Let rest for 5 minutes before slicing on the diagonal, against the grain, into thin strips.

Serve the steak alongside the slaw.

PER SERVING	
Calories	240
Calories from fat	60
Fat	6 g
Saturated fat	2.5 g
Trans fatty acids, total	0 g
Polyunsaturated fat	0.5 g
Monounsaturated fat	2.5 g
Cholesterol	60 mg
Sodium	940 mg
Carbohydrate	22 g
Dietary fiber	5 g
Sugars	13 g
Protein	26 g

TIP *A food processor can make prepping the slaw easier. Use the slicing blade for the cabbage, the shredding blade for the carrots, and the chopping blade for the garlic, shallot, jalapeño, mint, and cilantro. When using large amounts of fresh herbs, the thin stems can be used, but remove and discard the thicker stems.*

CHICKEN FAJITAS WITH TRICOLORED PEPPERS

Why go out for fajitas when you can make them at home for a fraction of the price you'd pay at a restaurant? They're simple to prepare and are particularly great for families—everyone can roll up their sleeves and create their own combinations. Let the veggies take center stage: use lots of onions and colorful peppers and supplement with the chicken.

4 SERVINGS

Juice of 2 limes

2 tablespoons canola oil, divided use

3 garlic cloves, smashed

1 teaspoon chili powder

1 teaspoon ground cumin

1 teaspoon paprika

1/2 teaspoon dried oregano

1/2 teaspoon salt

Pinch cayenne pepper

1 pound boneless, skinless chicken breasts, sliced into strips

1 large onion, sliced

1 large red onion, sliced

1 red bell pepper, seeded and sliced into strips

1 green bell pepper, seeded and sliced into strips

1 yellow or orange bell pepper, seeded and sliced into strips

8 (5- to 6-inch) whole wheat, flour, or corn tortillas

1 avocado, sliced into eighths

Salsa, sour cream, or shredded cheese, optional

In a zip-top bag or bowl, combine the lime juice, 1 tablespoon of the oil, garlic, chili powder, cumin, paprika, oregano, salt, and cayenne pepper. Add the chicken and stir to coat. Refrigerate for 30 minutes or more, turning occasionally if possible.

Preheat the oven to 350 degrees.

In a large skillet over medium-high heat, add the remaining 1 tablespoon of oil. Sauté the onions for 5 to 8 minutes, or until softened. Add the bell peppers and cook for 3 to 5 minutes. Remove the vegetables and set aside. Remove the chicken from the marinade, letting excess drip off, and sauté for 3 to 5 minutes. Reduce the heat to medium-low, return the vegetables to the skillet, and sauté for 1 to 2 minutes, or until the vegetables are heated through.

Meanwhile, wrap the tortillas in aluminum foil and bake for 10 minutes. (Tortillas can also be wrapped in a damp towel and warmed in the microwave on high for 15 to 30 seconds.)

Spoon the chicken mixture onto the tortillas and top with sliced avocado.

Serve with salsa, sour cream, or cheese, if desired.

PER SERVING

Calories	470
Calories from fat	160
Fat	18 g
Saturated fat	4.5 g
Trans fatty acids, total	0 g
Polyunsaturated fat	3 g
Monounsaturated fat	9 g
Cholesterol	65 mg
Sodium	400 mg
Carbohydrate	46 g
Dietary fiber	11 g
Sugars	10 g
Protein	32 g

For a vegetarian version, you can substitute portobello mushrooms for the chicken. Fish or shrimp also work well in this recipe. Throw in some poblanos or a jalapeño for added flavor.

SPICED SHRIMP WITH DRIED FRUIT COUSCOUS

This entrée combines Moroccan-inspired, fragrantly seasoned shrimp with fast-cooking couscous, currants, dried apricots, and dried cranberries. Adding dried fruit into dishes is a delicious way to add more fiber and nutrients. It's finished with a burst of citrus and fresh parsley to create a memorable touch.

4 SERVINGS

1 teaspoon ground ginger

1 teaspoon paprika

1 teaspoon ground cinnamon

1/4 teaspoon cayenne pepper

1 pound shrimp, peeled and deveined

Salt

1 tablespoon olive oil

1/4 onion, finely chopped

1 garlic clove, minced

2 cups reduced-sodium chicken or vegetable broth

1 1/2 cups whole wheat or regular couscous

1/4 cup chopped dried apricots

1/4 cup currants, raisins, or golden raisins

1/4 cup dried sweetened cranberries

Zest of 1 orange

2 tablespoons chopped fresh Italian parsley

In a bowl, combine the ginger, paprika, cinnamon, and cayenne pepper. Add the shrimp, sprinkle with salt, and stir to coat.

In a large skillet over medium heat, add the oil. Cook the shrimp (and any excess spice mixture) for 1 to 2 minutes per side, or until just cooked through. Remove the shrimp and set aside. Reduce the heat to medium, add the onion and garlic, and sauté for 2 to 3 minutes, or until softened. Add the broth and bring to a boil, stirring to dislodge any bits of food that might have stuck to the bottom of the skillet. Remove from the heat, add the couscous, apricots, currants, cranberries, and orange zest and stir to combine. Cover and let sit for 5 minutes. Return the shrimp to the skillet, add the parsley, and stir to combine.

PER SERVING	
Calories	470
Calories from fat	50
Fat	5 g
Saturated fat	1 g
Trans fatty acids, total	0 g
Polyunsaturated fat	1 g
Monounsaturated fat	3 g
Cholesterol	185 mg
Sodium	730 mg
Carbohydrate	72 g
Dietary fiber	8 g
Sugars	19 g
Protein	36 g

If you are watching your sodium intake, substitute homemade broth (page 206) for store-bought or make the couscous with water and season with salt, to taste.

LETTUCE WRAPS WITH TOFU AND VEGETABLES

This stir-fry is wrapped in lettuce leaves and eaten like a taco for a "hands-on" dining experience.

Tofu is the chameleon of proteins because it takes on the flavors used in the dish, making it important to use a super flavorful sauce like this one. Weighing down the tofu before cooking helps extract excess liquid, making it easier to cut and allowing it to hold its shape better during cooking.

4 SERVINGS

1 (16-ounce) block extra-firm tofu

1/4 cup smooth peanut butter, preferably all natural

3 tablespoons hoisin sauce

1 tablespoon reduced-sodium soy sauce

1 tablespoon honey

1 teaspoon dark sesame oil

1 teaspoon chili paste (sambal oelek)

1 tablespoon canola oil

3 garlic cloves, minced

1 (1-inch) piece peeled fresh ginger, minced

2 scallions, white and light green parts only, sliced

3 cups shredded cabbage or coleslaw mix

1 cup matchstick or grated carrots

2 red bell peppers, seeded and cut into thin strips

1 small head Boston or Bibb lettuce, leaves separated and core discarded

Line a plate with paper towels and place the tofu on top. Cover with paper towels and top with another plate weighed down with cans or a heavy pot for 30 minutes to release excess water. Pat dry and cut into 1-inch cubes.

Meanwhile, in a blender, combine the peanut butter, hoisin sauce, soy sauce, honey, sesame oil, and chili paste.

In a large, preferably nonstick, skillet over medium-high heat, add the oil. Cook the tofu for 1 to 2 minutes per side, or until golden brown. Remove the tofu and set aside. Add the garlic, ginger, and scallions and sauté for 1 minute. Add the cabbage, carrots, and bell peppers and sauté for 5 to 8 minutes, or until just tender. Reduce the heat to medium-low, return the tofu to the skillet, add the sauce, and sauté for 1 to 2 minutes, or until the tofu is heated through and coated with sauce.

Spoon the tofu mixture onto the lettuce leaves. Top with additional hoisin sauce, if desired.

PER SERVING	
Calories	350
Calories from fat	170
Fat	19 g
Saturated fat	3 g
Trans fatty acids, total	0 g
Polyunsaturated fat	7 g
Monounsaturated fat	8 g
Cholesterol	0 mg
Sodium	410 mg
Carbohydrate	30 g
Dietary fiber	7 g
Sugars	16 g
Protein	17 g

This dish can also be made with chicken, shrimp, or pork. If you can't find chili paste (sambal oelek), substitute chili garlic sauce or Sriracha.

SWEET CHILI FISH BURGERS WITH CILANTRO SLAW

A fish burger is a better burger, especially when it's flecked with ginger, cilantro, and sweet chili sauce and topped with a tangy slaw. Any white firm fish, such as cod, scrod, monkfish, sea bass, halibut, haddock, or snapper, will work in this recipe. Look for sweet chili sauce, fish sauce, chili garlic sauce, and panko (Japanese-style bread crumbs) in the international food aisle of your supermarket.

4 SERVINGS

SLAW

2 tablespoons fish sauce

2 tablespoons lime juice

1 teaspoon chili garlic sauce

$1/2$ teaspoon granulated sugar

4 cups (7 ounces) coleslaw mix

1 shallot, finely chopped

$1/2$ cup chopped fresh cilantro

BURGER

1 garlic clove

1 shallot

1 ($1/2$-inch) piece peeled fresh ginger

$1/4$ cup fresh cilantro

$1/2$ jalapeño pepper, seeded

1 egg

3 tablespoons sweet chili sauce

$1/2$ teaspoon salt

1 pound white fish fillet, such as cod, cut into 1-inch pieces

$1/3$ cup panko

1 tablespoon canola oil

4 whole wheat rolls, split and lightly toasted

FOR THE SLAW: In a bowl, combine the fish sauce, lime juice, chili garlic sauce, and sugar. Add the coleslaw mix, shallot, and cilantro and stir well to combine. Set aside.

FOR THE BURGERS: In a food processor, with the motor running, add the garlic, shallot, ginger, cilantro, and jalapeño. Scrape down the sides, add the egg, sweet chili sauce, and salt, and pulse to combine. Add the fish and pulse until coarsely chopped and the mixture just holds together. The fish should still be chunky. Transfer to a bowl, add the panko, and stir to combine. Form into four patties.

In a large, preferably nonstick, flat griddle or skillet over medium heat, add the oil. Cook the burgers for 4 to 5 minutes per side, or until the fish is cooked through and the tops and bottoms are golden brown and lightly crusted, pressing down with a spatula to help compress the burgers occasionally.

Serve the burgers on the rolls and top with the slaw.

PER SERVING

Calories	340
Calories from fat	70
Fat	8 g
Saturated fat	1 g
Trans fatty acids, total	0 g
Polyunsaturated fat	2.5 g
Monounsaturated fat	3.5 g
Cholesterol	95 mg
Sodium	1420 mg
Carbohydrate	40 g
Dietary fiber	6 g
Sugars	12 g
Protein	27 g

TIP *The burgers are a bit fragile, so make sure they're cooked through on the bottom before trying to flip them. Use a flat griddle or a skillet that's large enough for you to work the spatula around the burgers. Even if they break apart a little, no one will be the wiser once they're on the bun!*

SPAGHETTI WITH SPICY TOMATO AND OLIVE SAUCE

This sauce gets heat and bold flavor from a generous dose of crushed red pepper flakes and assertive ingredients such as anchovies, capers, and black olives. Use kalamata olives—not canned black olives—or another strongly flavored variety from a jar or antipasti bar.

If you are watching your sodium intake, choose no-salt-added tomatoes and reduce the anchovy paste, capers, and olives by half to start. Add more to taste, if needed.

4 SERVINGS

8 ounces whole wheat spaghetti or other pasta

2 tablespoons olive oil

4 garlic cloves, minced

1 teaspoon crushed red pepper flakes, or to taste

1 (28-ounce) can diced tomatoes

1 tablespoon anchovy paste or 2 anchovy fillets, drained and chopped

1 teaspoon dried oregano

1 teaspoon dried basil

1/4 cup capers, drained

15 pitted kalamata olives, chopped

Salt and freshly ground black pepper

1/4 cup freshly grated Parmesan cheese

Prepare the spaghetti according to the package directions for al dente (just firm).

Meanwhile, in a large skillet over medium heat, add the oil. Sauté the garlic and red pepper flakes for 1 minute. Add the tomatoes and their juice, anchovy paste, oregano, and basil and bring to a boil. Reduce the heat and simmer for 15 minutes, or until thickened, stirring occasionally. Add the capers and olives and simmer for 1 minute. If there's room in the skillet, add the pasta to the sauce and stir to combine. If not, place the pasta in a bowl and add the sauce. Season with salt and pepper and additional red pepper flakes, if desired. Top with the cheese.

PER SERVING

Calories	360
Calories from fat	120
Fat	14 g
Saturated fat	2 g
Trans fatty acids, total	0 g
Polyunsaturated fat	3 g
Monounsaturated fat	8 g
Cholesterol	5 mg
Sodium	820 mg
Carbohydrate	53 g
Dietary fiber	10 g
Sugars	6 g
Protein	13 g

 If you have fresh parsley or basil on hand, definitely throw in a few tablespoons at the end of the cooking. For more protein, add a can or two of tuna. If you don't have canned diced tomatoes, coarsely chop a can of whole tomatoes by hand or in a food processor.

EASY ONE-POT CHICKEN AND VEGETABLES

This simple dish is a fine example of "clean eating" without sacrificing flavor. There's nothing fancy or difficult, but each component maintains its integrity, resulting in a dish that is greater than the sum of its parts. Use fresh thyme if you can: it truly makes a difference.

Leeks can have grit in their root ends, so make sure to rinse well.

4 SERVINGS

- 4 boneless, skinless chicken breasts, pounded or sliced to even thickness
- Salt and freshly ground black pepper
- 2 tablespoons olive oil, divided use

- 16 small white mushrooms
- 16 baby carrots
- 2 leeks, white and light green parts only, halved and thickly sliced
- 2 celery stalks, cut into 1-inch pieces

- 2 garlic cloves, minced
- 2 sprigs fresh thyme, or 1 teaspoon dried thyme
- 1 cup reduced-sodium chicken broth

Sprinkle the chicken with salt and pepper.

In a large skillet over medium-high heat, add 1 tablespoon of the oil. Cook the chicken for 3 to 4 minutes per side, or until just cooked through and golden brown. Remove the chicken and set aside. Add the remaining 1 tablespoon of oil, mushrooms, carrots, leeks, celery, garlic, and thyme and sauté for 5 to 8 minutes, or until softened. Add the broth and bring to a boil, stirring to dislodge any bits of food that might have stuck to the bottom of the skillet. Reduce the heat, cover, and simmer for 15 minutes, stirring occasionally. Return the chicken and any accumulated juices to the skillet, cover, and cook for 1 to 2 minutes, or until the chicken is heated through. Remove the thyme sprigs before serving.

PER SERVING

Calories	310
Calories from fat	100
Fat	11 g
Saturated fat	2 g
Trans fatty acids, total	0 g
Polyunsaturated fat	2 g
Monounsaturated fat	6 g
Cholesterol	100 mg
Sodium	270 mg
Carbohydrate	13 g
Dietary fiber	3 g
Sugars	5 g
Protein	39 g

TIP *Always pat chicken dry with paper towels before searing for better browning. Don't overcrowd the pan, or the chicken will steam rather than brown.*

CHICKPEA BURGERS WITH RED PEPPER MAYO

These vegetarian burgers are a great way to use up leftover cooked brown rice by combining it with kitchen staples like carrots and canned chickpeas. Top with a dollop of dressed-up red pepper mayo and tuck the burgers into a whole wheat bun, pita or, for a truly low-cal meal, a fresh lettuce leaf.

If time allows, refrigerate the patties while preparing the side dishes to allow them time to firm up for easier cooking. For smaller appetites, make eight patties instead of four.

4 SERVINGS

MAYONNAISE

¼ cup chopped roasted red pepper, patted dry

¼ cup "light" or reduced-fat mayonnaise

⅛ teaspoon cayenne pepper

BURGERS

1 garlic clove

1 small shallot or 2 tablespoons chopped red onion

2 tablespoons finely chopped fresh Italian parsley

1 egg, beaten

1 (15.5-ounce) can chickpeas, rinsed, drained, and patted dry

1 cup cooked brown rice

1 carrot, grated

Salt and freshly ground black pepper

1 tablespoon canola oil

FOR THE MAYONNAISE: In a food processor, combine the roasted pepper, mayonnaise, and cayenne pepper until smooth. Transfer to a bowl.

FOR THE BURGERS: In a food processor with the motor running, add the garlic. Scrape down the sides, add the shallot and parsley, and pulse to combine. Add the egg, chickpeas, brown rice, and carrot and pulse until combined and moistened but still slightly chunky. Season with salt and pepper. Form into four patties.

In a large, preferably nonstick, skillet over medium heat, add the oil. Cook the burgers for 3 to 4 minutes per side, or until the tops and bottoms are golden brown and lightly crusted. Serve with a dollop of red pepper mayonnaise.

PER SERVING

Calories	260
Calories from fat	100
Fat	11 g
Saturated fat	1.5 g
Trans fatty acids, total	0 g
Polyunsaturated fat	4 g
Monounsaturated fat	4 g
Cholesterol	50 mg
Sodium	290 mg
Carbohydrate	34 g
Dietary fiber	7 g
Sugars	6 g
Protein	9 g

 TIP *If you want to roast your own red pepper, you can do it under the broiler, in a 500-degree oven, or over a gas flame on the stovetop. Cook the pepper until it's blackened on all sides, then wrap it in foil or place in a brown bag to steam and soften while it cools. When cool enough to handle, discard the skin, stem, and seeds.*

NOTES

SOUPS, SALADS, SANDWICHES, AND SMALL MEALS

DOUBLE CREAMY GRILLED CHEESE WITH APPLE

Transform a classic grilled cheese into something even creamier by using both goat cheese and Cheddar. Sandwiching thinly sliced apples between the layers of cheese adds sweetness and texture. For another unexpected twist, try using raisin bread or another dried fruit–flecked bread. Remember, all the ingredients enhance the finished product, so use a good hearty bread, sharp Cheddar, and a tasty apple.

1 SERVING

1/2 teaspoon "light" or reduced-fat mayonnaise

2 slices cinnamon-raisin or other fruit/nut bread

2 thin slices sharp Cheddar cheese or 1 (1-ounce) slice

1/4 cup (1 ounce) goat cheese, crumbled

4 very thin apple slices

Spread the mayonnaise on one side of each piece of bread and place on a plate, mayonnaise side down. Top one slice of the bread with one slice of Cheddar, half of the goat cheese, apple, and remaining goat and Cheddar cheeses (if only using one piece of Cheddar, layer Cheddar, apple, and then goat cheese). Top with the remaining slice of bread, dry side facing down.

Carefully place the sandwich in a skillet over medium heat. Cook until the bottom is golden and the cheese begins to melt, pressing down with a spatula to help the melted cheese adhere to the bread. Carefully turn the sandwich, and cook until the bottom is golden and the cheese has melted, pressing down with the spatula occasionally.

PER SERVING

Calories	330
Calories from fat	150
Fat	17 g
Saturated fat	9 g
Trans fatty acids, total	0.5 g
Polyunsaturated fat	1 g
Monounsaturated fat	4.5 g
Cholesterol	50 mg
Sodium	440 mg
Carbohydrate	34 g
Dietary fiber	3 g
Sugars	7 g
Protein	15 g

A chef's trick is to use mayonnaise instead of butter to coat the bread. It is easy to spread and has a higher smoke point than butter, making it less likely to burn before the inside is cooked through.

LICK-THE-BOWL-GOOD MUSHROOM SOUP

This soup is deceivingly rich and hearty. It's low in calories and fat and—because it's made without cream or dairy—it can easily be made vegan if you use vegetable broth. It is truly lick-the-bowl good!

For decadently rich mushroom flavor, top it with a drizzle of truffle oil. If you don't have it, the soup will still be delicious, but as my son said, "It takes it to the next level."

6 SERVINGS

2 tablespoons olive oil

2 leeks, white and light green parts only, halved lengthwise and sliced

2 carrots, chopped

1 onion, chopped

1 celery stalk, chopped

1 garlic clove, minced

2 pounds white mushrooms, coarsely chopped

2 sprigs fresh thyme

6 cups reduced-sodium chicken or vegetable broth

Salt and freshly ground black pepper

Truffle oil, optional

In a stockpot over medium heat, add the oil. Sauté the leeks, carrots, onion, and celery for 5 to 8 minutes, or until softened. Add the garlic and sauté for 1 minute. Add the mushrooms and thyme and sauté for 5 minutes. Add the broth and bring to a boil. Reduce the heat, cover, and simmer for 25 to 30 minutes, stirring occasionally. Discard the thyme sprigs.

Working in batches, transfer the soup to a blender or food processor, and let cool slightly before puréeing until smooth. Return to the stockpot and stir to combine over low heat. Season with salt and pepper. Drizzle individual servings with truffle oil, if desired.

PER SERVING	
Calories	130
Calories from fat	50
Fat	5 g
Saturated fat	0.5 g
Trans fatty acids, total	0 g
Polyunsaturated fat	1 g
Monounsaturated fat	3.5 g
Cholesterol	0 mg
Sodium	550 mg
Carbohydrate	15 g
Dietary fiber	3 g
Sugars	7 g
Protein	8 g

 You can also use the truffle oil for the Spinach and Mushroom Risotto (page 76).

FARRO SALAD WITH FETA AND FRESH HERBS

Grain salads are fiber- and nutrient-rich. But that's not their only benefit—they also taste delicious! Farro has a nutty flavor and toothsome texture, making it a good base for crunchy vegetables and protein-filled beans. Fresh herbs give this salad vibrancy.

7 SERVINGS

1 cup farro, rinsed

1/4 cup chopped fresh mint

1/4 cup chopped fresh Italian parsley

3 scallions, white and light green parts only, thinly sliced

1 carrot, chopped

1/2 cucumber, peeled, seeded, and chopped

1 (15-ounce) can chickpeas, rinsed and drained

1/2 cup crumbled feta cheese

1 tablespoon sherry vinegar

1 lemon, zested and juiced

3 tablespoons extra-virgin olive oil

Salt and freshly ground black pepper

In a saucepan, cover the farro with 2 inches of water and bring to a boil, stirring to combine. Skim any film that rises to the surface. Reduce the heat, cover, and simmer for 30 minutes, or until tender. Drain and pat dry.

Meanwhile, in a bowl, combine the mint, parsley, scallions, carrot, cucumber, chickpeas, and feta. Add the farro and stir to combine.

In a bowl, combine the vinegar, lemon juice, and zest. Slowly whisk in the oil to incorporate (or put into a jar and shake well). Drizzle the dressing over the salad to lightly coat, and stir gently to combine. Season with salt and pepper.

PER SERVING	
Calories	260
Calories from fat	90
Fat	10 g
Saturated fat	2.5 g
Trans fatty acids, total	0 g
Polyunsaturated fat	1.5 g
Monounsaturated fat	5 g
Cholesterol	10 mg
Sodium	190 mg
Carbohydrate	34 g
Dietary fiber	7 g
Sugars	3 g
Protein	9 g

For a more substantial meal, add canned tuna, cooked shrimp or chicken, or serve on top of a mixed salad. If you don't have farro, you can use barley, wheat berries, or quinoa.

ARUGULA AND KALE SALAD

Two assertive greens, arugula and kale, are paired in this flavorful salad. Really sear the mushrooms to give them a nice crust, and toss them with the greens while they are still warm. If mushrooms aren't your thing, leave them out.

Reducing balsamic vinegar concentrates its flavor and helps it coat the greens. Keep a measuring cup near the stove and as the vinegar thickens, transfer it to the cup to check its progress.

4 SERVINGS

1 cup white balsamic vinegar

1 tablespoon granulated sugar

1 teaspoon olive oil

8 ounces white mushrooms, sliced

4 cups arugula

4 cups kale, preferably Tuscan or lacinato, thick ribs removed, cut into 1-inch pieces

2 tablespoons extra-virgin olive oil

1 ounce (3 tablespoons) toasted almonds, chopped

1 ounce Parmesan cheese, freshly grated

Kosher or sea salt and freshly ground black pepper

In a small saucepan over medium-high heat, boil the vinegar and sugar for 15 to 25 minutes, or until syrupy and reduced to between $\frac{1}{3}$ and $\frac{1}{4}$ cup, swirling the pan occasionally. Set aside to cool. It will become thicker upon standing.

Meanwhile, in a skillet over high heat, add the oil. Sauté the mushrooms for 3 to 5 minutes, or until golden brown.

In a bowl, combine the arugula and kale. Using your hands, massage the greens with the extra-virgin olive oil. Drizzle with 2 tablespoons balsamic reduction, or to taste. Add the mushrooms, nuts, and Parmesan and stir to combine. Season with salt and pepper.

PER SERVING	
Calories	200
Calories from fat	130
Fat	14 g
Saturated fat	2.5 g
Trans fatty acids, total	0 g
Polyunsaturated fat	2 g
Monounsaturated fat	9 g
Cholesterol	5 mg
Sodium	135 mg
Carbohydrate	15 g
Dietary fiber	2 g
Sugars	11 g
Protein	7 g

 For added protein, serve with grilled fish or with quinoa.

STUFFED ROASTED VEGETABLE SANDWICH

When you have a group over for lunch, this sandwich will wow them. You can cook and assemble it beforehand to warm up later. Use whatever veggies you like or happen to have on hand.

To make room for the filling, discard the excess bread inside the loaf, leaving a thin shell of crust. The vegetables will shrink during cooking, so slice them more thickly than you think you should.

Use a serrated knife to cut the sandwich into wedges.

6 SERVINGS

1 pound eggplant, thickly sliced lengthwise

Salt

2 zucchini, thickly sliced lengthwise

1 red bell pepper, seeded and quartered

1 red onion, thickly sliced

2 portobello mushrooms, stemmed and cut crosswise into two rounds

1 tablespoon olive oil

1 (7- to 8-inch) round whole wheat or white bread loaf

2 tablespoons pesto

1 (4-ounce) ball fresh mozzarella, thinly sliced and patted dry

8 sun-dried tomatoes packed in oil, patted dry

Preheat the oven to 425 degrees.

In a large colander, sprinkle the eggplant slices with salt and set in the sink to drain for 10 minutes. Pat dry.

Meanwhile, lightly coat two foil-lined, rimmed baking sheets with nonstick cooking spray. Place the zucchini, bell pepper, onion, mushrooms, and eggplant in a single layer on the baking sheets. Brush with the oil and sprinkle with salt. Bake for 20 to 30 minutes, or until tender and slightly charred, flipping the vegetables every 10 minutes. Remove and reduce the oven temperature to 375 degrees.

Meanwhile, cut the bread in half and, using your fingers, remove the soft insides from the top and bottom, leaving a 1-inch-thick shell. Spread the pesto on both halves. On the bottom half, layer the mozzarella, roasted vegetables, and sun-dried tomatoes and top with the remaining bread.

Place a baking sheet weighed down with cans or a heavy pot on the sandwich for 20 to 30 minutes, pushing down occasionally to condense. Wrap the sandwich in aluminum foil and bake for 15 to 20 minutes, or until warm.

PER SERVING

Calories	300
Calories from fat	100
Fat	11 g
Saturated fat	4 g
Trans fatty acids, total	0 g
Polyunsaturated fat	1.5 g
Monounsaturated fat	4.5 g
Cholesterol	15 mg
Sodium	460 mg
Carbohydrate	39 g
Dietary fiber	7 g
Sugars	9 g
Protein	13 g

MEDITERRANEAN TUNA SALAD

The next time you think tuna, think "outside the can." This pantry staple is an economical protein choice, not just a banal sandwich filling to be smothered in mayonnaise. In this recipe, tuna is mixed with crunchy veggies, artichokes, olives, and a lemon-olive oil dressing for a change of pace.

Serve as is, on whole grain bread, or over a bed of baby spinach or greens.

4 SERVINGS

1 (6-ounce) can white tuna packed in water, drained

1 tomato, seeded and chopped

1 red bell pepper, seeded and chopped

1 carrot, chopped

1 celery stalk, chopped

1 scallion, white and light green parts only, thinly sliced

10 pitted kalamata olives, sliced

1 cup artichoke hearts, chopped

2 tablespoons chopped fresh Italian parsley

2 tablespoons fresh lemon juice

1 teaspoon Dijon mustard

2 tablespoons extra-virgin olive oil

Salt and freshly ground black pepper

In a bowl, flake the tuna. Add the tomato, bell pepper, carrot, celery, scallion, olives, artichoke hearts, and parsley and stir to combine.

In a bowl, combine the lemon juice and mustard. Slowly whisk in the oil to incorporate (or put into a jar and shake well). Drizzle the dressing over the salad to lightly coat and stir gently to combine. Season with salt and pepper.

PER SERVING

Calories	190
Calories from fat	100
Fat	11 g
Saturated fat	1.5 g
Trans fatty acids, total	0 g
Polyunsaturated fat	1.5 g
Monounsaturated fat	7 g
Cholesterol	15 mg
Sodium	430 mg
Carbohydrate	12 g
Dietary fiber	5 g
Sugars	4 g
Protein	11 g

 For more protein, add another can of tuna, cooked beans, or hard-boiled eggs. You can also add anchovies if you're a fan.

BARBECUE CHICKEN SANDWICHES

Who knew barbecue flavor could be this easy? Making homemade barbecue sauce takes only ten minutes and allows you to control the ingredients that go into it, so you can avoid excess sugar.

4 SERVINGS

¹/₂ cup ketchup

2 tablespoons apple cider vinegar

1 tablespoon Worcestershire sauce

1 tablespoon light or dark brown sugar

1 tablespoon molasses

1 garlic clove, minced

¹/₂ teaspoon paprika

¹/₂ teaspoon dry mustard

2 to 3 shakes hot sauce, or to taste

3 cups shredded cooked chicken breast

Salt and freshly ground black pepper

4 whole wheat rolls, split and lightly toasted

In a large saucepan over medium-low heat, simmer the ketchup, vinegar, Worcestershire sauce, brown sugar, molasses, garlic, paprika, mustard, and hot sauce for 10 minutes, stirring frequently. Add the chicken and cook for 1 to 2 minutes, stirring to combine. Season with salt and pepper and additional hot sauce, if desired.

Divide the chicken on the rolls.

PER SERVING

Calories	350
Calories from fat	50
Fat	6 g
Saturated fat	1.5 g
Trans fatty acids, total	0 g
Polyunsaturated fat	2 g
Monounsaturated fat	2 g
Cholesterol	90 mg
Sodium	630 mg
Carbohydrate	38 g
Dietary fiber	4 g
Sugars	17 g
Protein	37 g

TIP *For a treat, top the chicken with Honey Coleslaw (page 146) or serve the coleslaw on the side.*

WHITE BEAN, JALAPEÑO, AND KALE SOUP

A couple of diced jalapeños give this soup unexpected heat, and carrots and kale provide heft. If possible, use Tuscan kale (also known as lacinato kale). Trim and discard the thicker stems and ribs before chopping. If you don't have time to presoak the beans, you can substitute two cans of navy or cannellini beans.

6 SERVINGS

1 cup dried white beans

1 tablespoon canola oil

2 jalapeño peppers, seeded and finely chopped

1 onion, chopped

1 celery stalk, chopped

6 cups reduced-sodium chicken or vegetable broth

3 carrots, cut into 1-inch pieces

4 cups chopped kale, preferably Tuscan or lacinato, thick ribs removed

Salt and freshly ground black pepper

In a bowl, cover the beans with 3 inches of water and soak overnight. Drain.

In a stockpot over medium-high heat, add the oil. Sauté the jalapeños, onion, and celery for 5 to 8 minutes, or until softened. Add the broth and bring to a boil. Add the beans and stir to combine. Reduce the heat, cover, and simmer for 45 to 60 minutes, or until the beans are tender, stirring occasionally. Add the carrots and kale and stir to combine. Cook for 15 minutes, or until the vegetables are tender. Season with salt and pepper.

PER SERVING

Calories	180
Calories from fat	25
Fat	3 g
Saturated fat	0.5 g
Trans fatty acids, total	0 g
Polyunsaturated fat	1 g
Monounsaturated fat	1.5 g
Cholesterol	0 mg
Sodium	550 mg
Carbohydrate	29 g
Dietary fiber	7 g
Sugars	5 g
Protein	12 g

For a thicker soup, purée a few cups in a blender or with an immersion blender before adding the carrots. For an even heartier soup, add some cooked chicken at the end.

SPINACH SALAD WITH SQUASH AND GOAT CHEESE

This autumnal salad makes a great main course or a substantial side dish when paired with simply prepared fish or chicken.

Reducing the apple cider concentrates its flavor. Keep a measuring cup near the stove and as the cider thickens, transfer the mixture to the cup to check its progress.

4 SERVINGS

1 small or $\frac{1}{2}$ large butternut squash (about 1 pound), peeled, seeded, and cut into $\frac{3}{4}$-inch cubes

1 tablespoon olive oil

Salt and freshly ground black pepper

$\frac{1}{2}$ cup wheat berries or farro

$\frac{1}{2}$ cup apple cider

2 tablespoons apple cider vinegar

$\frac{1}{2}$ shallot, finely chopped

$\frac{1}{2}$ teaspoon whole grain or Dijon mustard

$\frac{1}{2}$ teaspoon honey

2 tablespoons extra-virgin olive oil

1 (5- to 6-ounce) package fresh baby spinach, arugula, baby kale, or spring mix

$\frac{1}{4}$ cup dried sweetened cranberries

$\frac{1}{2}$ cup (2 ounces) crumbled goat cheese

$\frac{1}{4}$ cup pomegranate seeds

Preheat the oven to 400 degrees.

Lightly coat a foil-lined, rimmed baking sheet with nonstick cooking spray. Place the squash on the baking sheet and drizzle with the olive oil. Sprinkle with salt and pepper and stir to coat. Evenly distribute the squash on the baking sheet. Roast for 20 to 30 minutes, or until tender and slightly charred, stirring the squash every 10 minutes.

Meanwhile, in a saucepan, cover the wheat berries with 2 inches water and bring to a boil, stirring to combine. Skim any film that rises to the surface. Reduce the heat, cover, and simmer for 15 to 20 minutes, or until tender. Drain and pat dry.

In a saucepan over medium-high heat, boil the apple cider, vinegar, and shallot until the mixture reduces to $\frac{1}{4}$ cup. Transfer to a bowl, add the mustard and honey, and slowly whisk in the extra-virgin olive oil to incorporate (or put into a jar and shake well). Season with salt and pepper.

In a bowl, combine the spinach, cranberries, and squash. Drizzle the dressing over the salad to lightly coat and stir gently to combine (you might not need all the dressing). Top with the wheat berries, goat cheese, and pomegranate seeds.

PER SERVING

Calories	290
Calories from fat	130
Fat	14 g
Saturated fat	3.5 g
Trans fatty acids, total	0 g
Polyunsaturated fat	1.5 g
Monounsaturated fat	8 g
Cholesterol	15 mg
Sodium	95 mg
Carbohydrate	37 g
Dietary fiber	7 g
Sugars	12 g
Protein	7 g

KALE, APPLE, AND BRUSSELS SPROUT SALAD

This refreshing no-cook salad should appeal to those looking to incorporate more raw foods into their diet. It might be a surprise that you can eat Brussels sprouts without cooking them, but like cabbage, they can be eaten both raw and cooked.

Choose a sweet, semifirm apple you like to eat on its own and Tuscan kale (also known as lacinato kale) if possible. With kale, it's important to tenderize the greens by rubbing the dressing into the leaves to better penetrate them.

6 SERVINGS

- 4 ounces kale, preferably Tuscan or lacinato, thick ribs removed
- 4 ounces Brussels sprouts, trimmed and halved
- 1 large apple, cored and quartered
- 1 lemon, zested and juiced
- 1 tablespoon minced shallot
- 1 teaspoon Dijon mustard
- 1 teaspoon granulated sugar
- 2 tablespoons extra-virgin olive oil
- Salt and freshly ground black pepper

In a food processor fitted with a thin slicing blade, slice the kale, Brussels sprouts, and apple (you might need to do this in batches). Transfer to a bowl.

In a bowl, combine the lemon juice, zest, shallot, mustard, and sugar. Slowly whisk in the oil to incorporate (or put into a jar and shake well). Drizzle the dressing over the kale mixture and massage the dressing into the greens with your fingers. Season with salt and pepper.

PER SERVING	
Calories	80
Calories from fat	45
Fat	5 g
Saturated fat	0.5 g
Trans fatty acids, total	0 g
Polyunsaturated fat	0.5 g
Monounsaturated fat	3.5 g
Cholesterol	0 mg
Sodium	35 mg
Carbohydrate	10 g
Dietary fiber	2 g
Sugars	6 g
Protein	2 g

 TIP *If you are looking for more ways to incorporate raw foods into your diet, also try the Carrot and Beet Salad (page 147).*

CARROT AND PARSNIP SOUP TWO WAYS

For many people, the parsnip joins rutabagas and turnips in the category of daunting and mysterious-looking root-vegetables. But the parsnip, which resembles a white carrot, should be appreciated for its sweet and starchy qualities. It provides body and depth to this carrot soup, in addition to potassium, antioxidants, and fiber.

The stovetop soup is a little more refined than the roasted variation, which has the added intensity of flavors from roasting.

STOVETOP CARROT AND PARSNIP SOUP

Use a food processor to chop the vegetables for shorter prep time. They don't have to be exactly even because they are puréed after cooking. Chop the onion first by using the pulse button. Remove it and then coarsely chop the carrots and parsnips in the machine.

If you have fresh chives on hand, sprinkle them on top before serving.

6 SERVINGS

1 tablespoon canola oil

1 onion, chopped

1 pound carrots, chopped

1 pound parsnips, chopped

5 to 6 cups reduced-sodium chicken or vegetable broth

Salt and freshly ground black pepper

Sliced fresh chives, optional

In a stockpot over medium heat, add the oil. Sauté the onion for 5 to 8 minutes, or until softened. Add the carrots and parsnips and stir to combine. Add 5 cups of broth and bring to a boil. Reduce the heat, cover, and simmer for 20 to 30 minutes, or until the vegetables are very tender, stirring occasionally.

Working in batches, transfer to a blender or food processor and let cool slightly before puréeing until smooth. Return to the stockpot over low heat and stir to combine. If the soup is too thick, add broth. Season with salt and pepper and top with chives, if desired.

PER SERVING	
Calories	120
Calories from fat	25
Fat	2.5 g
Saturated fat	0 g
Trans fatty acids, total	0 g
Polyunsaturated fat	1 g
Monounsaturated fat	1.5 g
Cholesterol	0 mg
Sodium	480 mg
Carbohydrate	21 g
Dietary fiber	5 g
Sugars	8 g
Protein	4 g

ROASTED CARROT AND PARSNIP SOUP

If you want a deeper vegetable flavor with a sweet note of caramelization, roast your veggies before adding them to the broth. It's a truly hands-free way of cooking!

6 SERVINGS

1 onion, cut into 1-inch pieces

1 pound carrots, cut into 1-inch pieces

1 pound parsnips, cut into 1-inch pieces

1 tablespoon olive oil

Salt and freshly ground black pepper

5 to 6 cups reduced-sodium chicken or vegetable broth

Preheat the oven to 400 degrees.

Lightly coat a foil-lined, rimmed baking sheet with nonstick cooking spray. Place the onion, carrots, and parsnips on the baking sheet and drizzle with the oil. Sprinkle with salt and pepper and stir to coat. Evenly distribute the vegetables on the baking sheet. Roast for 30 to 40 minutes, or until tender and slightly charred, stirring the vegetables every 10 minutes.

Transfer to a blender or food processor and add 2 cups of broth. Purée until very smooth. Transfer to a stockpot, add 3 cups of broth, and bring to a boil. Reduce the heat and simmer for 5 minutes, or until heated through, stirring to combine. If the soup is too thick, add broth. Season with salt and pepper.

PER SERVING

Calories	120
Calories from fat	25
Fat	2.5 g
Saturated fat	0.5 g
Trans fatty acids, total	0 g
Polyunsaturated fat	0.5 g
Monounsaturated fat	1.5 g
Cholesterol	0 mg
Sodium	480 mg
Carbohydrate	21 g
Dietary fiber	5 g
Sugars	8 g
Protein	4 g

GREENS WITH CHICKEN, APPLE, AND BLUE CHEESE

A truly memorable salad includes a variety of tastes and textures. This salad does that by combining pungent blue cheese; chewy, dried cranberries; and a crunchy, sweet apple with a bright acidic dressing. Choose a sweet but semifirm apple you would eat on its own.

Buy a premade spring lettuce mix or make your own, combining arugula, kale, endive, and/or leafy lettuces. For variety, instead of an apple, substitute a pear or grapes.

4 SERVINGS

1/2 shallot, finely chopped

1 tablespoon sherry vinegar

1 tablespoon fresh lemon juice

1/2 teaspoon Dijon mustard

1/2 teaspoon granulated sugar

2 tablespoons extra-virgin olive oil

Salt and freshly ground black pepper

8 cups lettuce mix

2 cups chopped cooked chicken breast

1 large apple, cored and cut into 1/2-inch pieces

1/2 cup chopped fresh Italian parsley

1/3 cup crumbled blue cheese

2 tablespoons dried sweetened cranberries

In a bowl, combine the shallot and vinegar and let sit for 5 minutes. Add the lemon juice, mustard, and sugar and stir to combine. Slowly whisk in the oil to incorporate (or put into a jar and shake well). Season with salt and pepper.

In a bowl, combine the lettuce, chicken, apple, parsley, blue cheese, and cranberries. Drizzle the dressing over the greens to lightly coat and stir gently to combine.

PER SERVING

Calories	280
Calories from fat	120
Fat	13 g
Saturated fat	4 g
Trans fatty acids, total	0 g
Polyunsaturated fat	1.5 g
Monounsaturated fat	7 g
Cholesterol	70 mg
Sodium	260 mg
Carbohydrate	15 g
Dietary fiber	2 g
Sugars	10 g
Protein	26 g

GREEK PITA "TACO"

Who doesn't love a hummus and Greek salad pita sandwich? But let's be honest: it can be hard to evenly distribute the ingredients into a split pita half. Separating the pita around its edge and gently prying it apart so that you can form a pita "taco" makes every bite better. Use the hummus as the "glue" to hold everything together.

Use store-bought hummus or try the Roasted Carrot Hummus (page 177).

2 SERVINGS

1 cup chopped lettuce or lettuce mix

10 pitted kalamata olives, sliced

1/2 tomato, seeded and chopped

1/4 cucumber, peeled, seeded, and chopped

1/4 cup shredded or chopped carrots

3 tablespoons crumbled feta cheese

1 teaspoon chopped fresh dill, optional

2 teaspoons extra-virgin olive oil

2 teaspoons red wine vinegar

1/4 teaspoon celery seeds

Salt and freshly ground black pepper

1 whole wheat or plain pita

1/4 cup hummus

In a bowl, combine the lettuce, olives, tomato, cucumber, carrots, feta, and dill, if desired.

In a bowl, combine the oil, vinegar, and celery seeds (or put into a jar and shake well). Drizzle the dressing over the salad to lightly coat and stir gently to combine. Season with salt and pepper.

Microwave the pita on high for 10 seconds, or until just warmed. Split it around the edges into two large rounds and place it rough side up. Spread each piece with half of the hummus. Top with half of the salad. Fold the pita in half and eat like a taco.

PER SERVING	
Calories	270
Calories from Fat	150
Fat	16 g
Saturated fat	4 g
Trans fatty acids, total	0 g
Polyunsaturated fat	2.5 g
Monounsaturated fat	9 g
Cholesterol	15 mg
Sodium	650 mg
Carbohydrate	25 g
Dietary fiber	6 g
Sugars	5 g
Protein	8 g

TIP *For a change of pace, toss the salad with the dressing used in the Lentil Salad with Tahini Dressing (page 117).*

GREEN GODDESS SALMON SALAD

Homemade green goddess dressing, made with avocado, fresh herbs, and mayonnaise, adds creamy goodness to salads and crudités. Bookmark this recipe (and Lemony Tilapia with Butter Lettuce and Herbs on page 122) when you have an assortment of fresh herbs to use.

The salmon can be cooked a day ahead and refrigerated. You can also use leftover fish from a previous meal.

4 SERVINGS

1 pound salmon fillets

1 teaspoon olive oil

Salt and freshly ground black pepper

8 cups lettuce mix

1/2 cucumber, peeled, seeded, and chopped

1 cup cherry or grape tomatoes, halved

1 cup coarsely chopped artichoke hearts

1/2 cup chickpeas, rinsed and drained

1/2 avocado

3 tablespoons chopped fresh herbs, such as tarragon, basil, Italian parsley, and dill

2 tablespoons "light" or reduced-fat mayonnaise

2 to 3 tablespoons nonfat plain Greek yogurt or regular or reduced-fat sour cream

2 tablespoons fresh lemon juice

1 teaspoon anchovy paste or 1 minced anchovy fillet

1 scallion, white and light green parts only, sliced

Salt and freshly ground black pepper

Preheat the oven to 450 degrees.

Lightly coat a foil-lined, rimmed baking sheet with nonstick cooking spray. Place the salmon skin side down on the baking sheet. Brush with the olive oil and sprinkle with salt and pepper. Bake for 13 to 18 minutes, or until the fish is cooked through. Set aside to cool briefly and remove the skin. Transfer to a bowl and flake into bite-sized pieces.

Meanwhile, in a bowl, combine the lettuce, cucumber, tomatoes, artichokes, and chickpeas. Add the salmon and stir to combine.

In a food processor or blender, combine the avocado, herbs, mayonnaise, 2 tablespoons of the yogurt, lemon juice, anchovy paste, and scallion until smooth. Season with salt and pepper. If the dressing is too thick, add the remaining tablespoon of yogurt.

Drizzle the dressing over the salad to lightly coat and stir gently to combine (you might not need all the dressing). Serve remaining dressing on the side, if desired.

PER SERVING	
Calories	310
Calories from fat	130
Fat	14 g
Saturated fat	2.5 g
Trans fatty acids, total	0 g
Polyunsaturated fat	4 g
Monounsaturated fat	6 g
Cholesterol	65 mg
Sodium	320 mg
Carbohydrate	17 g
Dietary fiber	7 g
Sugars	5 g
Protein	29 g

CHUNKY PASTA AND BEAN SOUP

This soup, inspired by the classic Italian dish pasta e fagioli, is loaded with pasta, white beans, and greens. Traditionally, pancetta is used as a base, but even without it, the soup is a rich and comforting meal on a winter night. Serve with a big salad and toasted slices of Italian bread rubbed with garlic and drizzled with olive oil.

Increase the amounts of vegetables if you want a more veggie-centric soup. By cooking the soup and pasta separately, you can control how much pasta there is in each serving. If you'd like a thicker, more porridge-like consistency, cook the pasta directly in the soup.

6 SERVINGS

1 tablespoon olive oil

1 onion, chopped

2 carrots, chopped

1 celery stalk, chopped

2 garlic cloves, minced

1 teaspoon dried basil

1 teaspoon dried oregano

1 teaspoon dried thyme

1/2 teaspoon dried rosemary

6 cups reduced-sodium chicken or vegetable broth

1 (14.5-ounce) can diced tomatoes, drained

1 (15-ounce) can cannellini or white beans, rinsed and drained

3 cups coarsely chopped escarole, Swiss chard, or baby spinach

1 cup ditalini or other small pasta

Freshly grated Parmesan cheese, optional

In a stockpot over medium heat, add the oil. Sauté the onion, carrots, and celery for 5 to 8 minutes, or until softened. Add the garlic, basil, oregano, thyme, and rosemary and sauté for 1 minute. Add the broth and tomatoes and bring to a boil. Reduce the heat and simmer for 10 to 15 minutes, stirring occasionally. Add the beans and escarole and cook for 3 to 5 minutes, stirring to combine.

Meanwhile, in a saucepan, prepare the ditalini according to the package directions for al dente (just firm). Add the pasta to individual bowls of soup. Serve with cheese, if desired.

PER SERVING

Calories	220
Calories from fat	30
Fat	3 g
Saturated fat	0.5 g
Trans fatty acids, total	0 g
Polyunsaturated fat	0.5 g
Monounsaturated fat	1.5 g
Cholesterol	0 mg
Sodium	640 mg
Carbohydrate	39 g
Dietary fiber	6 g
Sugars	5 g
Protein	11 g

 TIP *As a guide, 1 tablespoon of oil should coat the bottom of your skillet or stockpot.*

CHICKEN AND ROASTED GRAPE TARTINES

When you want your chicken salad sandwich to stand out, try an open-faced version, also known as a tartine. Roasted grapes take it to the next level. Just be vigilant when they are roasting: as the sugar caramelizes, it quickly darkens, so you need to watch them closely to prevent burning. Shaking the pan frequently and lining your baking sheet with parchment paper will help protect the grapes and prevent a mess. (If you are pressed for time, skip the roasting and use halved raw grapes in the salad.)

4 SERVINGS

2 cups red seedless grapes

2 cups chopped cooked chicken breast

1 celery stalk, chopped

3 tablespoons "light" or reduced-fat mayonnaise

1 tablespoon thinly sliced fresh chives or 1 scallion, thinly sliced

1 tablespoon chopped fresh tarragon, Italian parsley, or basil

Salt and freshly ground black pepper

1/4 cup slivered or chopped toasted almonds

4 thick slices bakery-quality whole wheat bread, lightly toasted

Preheat the oven to 400 degrees.

Line a rimmed baking sheet with parchment paper and top with the grapes. Roast for 20 to 30 minutes, or until the juices release and the grapes have shrunk significantly, shaking the pan every 5 minutes to prevent burning. Set aside to cool briefly.

Meanwhile, in a bowl, combine the chicken, celery, mayonnaise, and chives. Add the tarragon and stir gently to combine. Season with salt and pepper. Add the grapes and almonds and stir gently to combine. Divide on bread and serve open faced.

PER SERVING	
Calories	360
Calories from fat	100
Fat	11 g
Saturated fat	1.5 g
Trans fatty acids, total	0 g
Polyunsaturated fat	3.5 g
Monounsaturated fat	4 g
Cholesterol	60 mg
Sodium	360 mg
Carbohydrate	38 g
Dietary fiber	5 g
Sugars	17 g
Protein	30 g

 TIP *Choose a thick-cut multigrain bread that can stand up to the chicken salad.*

LENTIL SALAD WITH TAHINI DRESSING

In this recipe, lentils are mixed into a brown rice pilaf for a filling and unexpected combination, an especially good option for vegetarians and vegans (when made with vegetable broth or water).

Tahini, a paste made of ground sesame seeds, provides a slight nutty flavor to the dressing. A little goes a long way, so use it sparingly and dilute with water and fresh lemon juice. Try the dressing in the Greek Pita "Taco" (page 112) for variety.

This salad can be served warm, at room temperature, or chilled.

6 SERVINGS

1 tablespoon canola oil

1/2 onion, chopped

1/2 carrot, chopped

1/2 celery stalk, chopped

1 garlic clove, minced

1 cup brown basmati rice

3 cups reduced-sodium chicken or vegetable broth or water

1/2 cup lentils, preferably French green (Lentilles du Puy)

3 tablespoons fresh lemon juice

2 tablespoons tahini, stirred well

2 tablespoons water

1 to 2 shakes Sriracha or other hot sauce, or to taste

Salt and freshly ground black pepper

In a saucepan over medium heat, add the oil. Sauté the onion, carrot, and celery for 3 to 5 minutes. Add the garlic and sauté for 1 minute. Add the rice and sauté for 1 minute. Add the broth and bring to a boil. Add the lentils and stir to combine. Reduce the heat to low, cover, and cook for 45 to 55 minutes, or until the liquid has absorbed and the rice and lentils are tender. Transfer to a bowl and let cool slightly.

In a bowl, combine the lemon juice, tahini, water, and Sriracha. Drizzle over the rice mixture and stir gently to combine. Season with salt and pepper.

PER SERVING

Calories	230
Calories from fat	60
Fat	6 g
Saturated fat	1 g
Trans fatty acids, total	0 g
Polyunsaturated fat	2.5 g
Monounsaturated fat	3 g
Cholesterol	0 mg
Sodium	270 mg
Carbohydrate	35 g
Dietary fiber	6 g
Sugars	3 g
Protein	9 g

Lentils, a fast-cooking legume, are a good and inexpensive source of protein and fiber, and also provide folate, iron, phosphorus, and potassium. Small green lentils, also known as French lentils or Lentilles du Puy, hold their texture well, making them a good option for this salad.

CHICKEN SANDWICHES WITH AVOCADO SALSA

Perk up a plain grilled chicken sandwich with an unexpected relish made with avocado and roasted jalapeños. Broiling the jalapeños adds a little smokiness to the mixture.

Many markets sell thin-sliced chicken cutlets. If not, just cut one large or two small boneless, skinless chicken breasts into thin slices.

3 SERVINGS

- 2 jalapeño peppers, halved and seeded
- 3 boneless, skinless chicken breast cutlets
- 2 tablespoons fresh lime juice
- 1 tablespoon extra-virgin olive oil
- 1 avocado, cut into $1/2$-inch pieces
- 1 tablespoon chopped fresh cilantro
- Salt and freshly ground black pepper
- 3 whole wheat rolls, split and lightly toasted

Preheat the broiler to high and set an oven rack 3 to 4 inches from the heat. Lightly coat a foil-lined, rimmed baking sheet or broiler pan with nonstick cooking spray. Place the jalapeños on the baking sheet. Broil for 1 to 2 minutes per side, or until blackened in spots. Wrap in the foil and set aside to cool briefly. Coarsely chop, discarding excess blackened skin.

Meanwhile, preheat a grill pan over medium-high heat and lightly coat with nonstick cooking spray. Cook the chicken for 2 to 3 minutes per side, or until just cooked through.

In a bowl, combine the lime juice and olive oil. Add the avocado, cilantro, and jalapeño and stir gently to combine. Season with salt and pepper.

Serve the chicken on the rolls, topped with the salsa.

PER SERVING	
Calories	400
Calories from fat	150
Fat	17 g
Saturated fat	3 g
Trans fatty acids, total	0 g
Polyunsaturated fat	3 g
Monounsaturated fat	10 g
Cholesterol	75 mg
Sodium	250 mg
Carbohydrate	30 g
Dietary fiber	7 g
Sugars	6 g
Protein	33 g

 If you feel like a splurge, melt cheese on half of the roll. If you are watching carbs, scoop out the excess bread from the top of the roll to make extra room for the salsa.

QUINOA SALAD WITH CRANBERRIES AND MINT

Quick-cooking quinoa is a grain-like seed that's high in protein, fiber, and essential amino acids. In this colorful combination, sweet dried fruit and savory mint and pistachios combine to make a wonderful small meal or a side for a simple roast chicken or other meat or fish entrée. It's also wonderful topped with grilled shrimp!

It's important to rinse quinoa before cooking, as the seeds are coated with saponins, natural chemical compounds that can be bitter.

5 SERVINGS

1 cup quinoa, rinsed and drained

2 cups water

2 scallions, white and light green parts only, thinly sliced

1/4 cup dried sweetened cranberries

1/4 cup golden raisins

3 tablespoons chopped fresh mint

2 tablespoons extra-virgin olive oil

2 tablespoons fresh lemon juice

Salt and freshly ground black pepper

1/4 cup chopped pistachios

In a saucepan, combine the quinoa and water and bring to a boil. Reduce the heat, stir to combine, cover, and simmer for 15 to 20 minutes, or until tender and the liquid is absorbed.

In a bowl, combine the quinoa, scallions, cranberries, raisins, and mint.

In a bowl, combine the oil and lemon juice (or put into a jar and shake well). Drizzle the dressing over the salad to lightly coat and stir gently to combine. Season with salt and pepper. Top with the pistachios.

PER SERVING	
Calories	260
Calories from fat	90
Fat	10 g
Saturated fat	1.5 g
Trans fatty acids, total	0 g
Polyunsaturated fat	3 g
Monounsaturated fat	6 g
Cholesterol	0 mg
Sodium	15 mg
Carbohydrate	38 g
Dietary fiber	5 g
Sugars	11 g
Protein	7 g

 TIP *Don't overload salads with heavy dressings. Using less dressing saves calories and lets you taste what you are eating.*

CHICKEN SOUP WITH MEATBALLS AND GREENS

This version of the classic Italian wedding soup gets a healthy makeover by using ground chicken in the meatballs and baking rather than frying them. For even better flavor, make your own broth (page 206).

Cooking the pasta and soup separately will keep the pasta from over-absorbing the broth if you have leftovers. If you'd like a thicker consistency, you can cook the pasta directly in the soup.

6 SERVINGS

MEATBALLS

1 egg

1/2 cup fresh bread crumbs

2 tablespoons low-fat milk

1/4 cup freshly grated Parmesan cheese

2 tablespoons finely chopped onion

2 tablespoons finely chopped fresh Italian parsley

1 garlic clove, minced

1 pound ground chicken or turkey breast

SOUP

1 tablespoon olive oil

1 onion, chopped

2 carrots, sliced 1/4-inch thick

2 celery stalks, sliced 1/4-inch thick

2 garlic cloves, minced

8 cups reduced-sodium chicken broth

1 (5- to 6-ounce) package fresh baby spinach

Salt and freshly ground black pepper

1/4 cup orzo or other small pasta

FOR THE MEATBALLS: Preheat the oven to 350 degrees. Lightly coat two foil-lined, rimmed baking sheets with nonstick cooking spray.

In a bowl, beat the egg. Add the bread crumbs and milk and stir to combine. Add the cheese, onion, parsley, and garlic and stir to combine. Add the chicken and stir gently to combine. Working with moistened hands, form the mixture into 1-inch balls and place on the baking sheets. Bake for 20 to 25 minutes, or until golden and cooked through.

FOR THE SOUP: Meanwhile, in a stockpot over medium heat, add the oil. Sauté the onion, carrots, and celery for 5 to 8 minutes, or until softened. Add the garlic and sauté for 1 minute. Add the broth and bring to a boil. Reduce the heat and simmer for 20 minutes, stirring occasionally. Add the meatballs and spinach and stir to combine. Season with salt and pepper.

In a saucepan, prepare the orzo according to the package directions for al dente (just firm). Add the pasta to individual bowls of soup.

PER SERVING

Calories	220
Calories from fat	50
Fat	5 g
Saturated fat	1.5 g
Trans fatty acids, total	0 g
Polyunsaturated fat	1 g
Monounsaturated fat	2.5 g
Cholesterol	75 mg
Sodium	860 mg
Carbohydrate	16 g
Dietary fiber	2 g
Sugars	5 g
Protein	26 g

LEMONY TILAPIA WITH BUTTER LETTUCE AND HERBS

This is the meal to turn to when you want something light but still satisfying. Use any combination of lettuces you prefer, or try a mesclun or spring mix. Fresh herbs really make this dish, so don't be afraid to use them generously.

For poaching the fish, use a white wine you would enjoy on its own. Chardonnay, pinot grigio, or sauvignon blanc all would work well.

4 SERVINGS

- 1 pound tilapia fillets
- 1/2 to 3/4 cup dry white wine
- 1 lemon, zested and juiced, divided use
- 1 teaspoon plus 2 tablespoons extra-virgin olive oil, divided use
- Salt and freshly ground black pepper
- 1 shallot, minced
- 1 tablespoon white vinegar
- 1 head butter lettuce, torn into bite-sized pieces
- 1 head endive, thinly sliced
- 1 head radicchio, thinly sliced
- 1 cup finely chopped fresh herbs, such as Italian parsley, dill, chives, or basil
- 2 tablespoons capers, drained

Preheat the oven to 400 degrees.

Place the fish in a baking pan. Add enough wine to reach halfway up the sides of the fish. Sprinkle with lemon zest, drizzle with 1 teaspoon of the oil, and season with salt and pepper. Bake for 10 to 12 minutes, or until the fish is cooked through. Remove the fish from the pan and set aside to cool briefly.

Meanwhile, in a bowl, combine the shallot and vinegar and let sit for 5 minutes. Add 2 tablespoons of the lemon juice. Slowly whisk in the remaining 2 tablespoons of the oil to incorporate (or put into a jar and shake well).

In a bowl, combine the lettuce, endive, radicchio, herbs, and capers. Drizzle the dressing over the salad to lightly coat and stir gently to combine (you might not need all the dressing). Season with salt and pepper and additional lemon juice, if desired. Top with the tilapia.

PER SERVING	
Calories	220
Calories from fat	80
Fat	9 g
Saturated fat	2 g
Trans fatty acids, total	0 g
Polyunsaturated fat	1.5 g
Monounsaturated fat	5 g
Cholesterol	50 mg
Sodium	200 mg
Carbohydrate	8 g
Dietary fiber	4 g
Sugars	1 g
Protein	25 g

 TIP *Growing your own herbs is a money-saving and healthy venture. When the weather is mild, plant mixed herbs in a few decorative pots and place them outside. In the cooler months, place a few small pots of your favorite herbs on your kitchen windowsill.*

PAN-BAGNAT "LITE"

This healthier version of the classic French sandwich pan-bagnat features tuna and hard-boiled eggs. For ease of preparation, store-bought tapenade (a spread typically made of olives, capers, anchovies, and olive oil), substitutes for the customary olives and anchovies. In a traditional pan-bagnat, the bread is soaked with olive oil. Here, a moderate amount of olive oil is added to the tuna. If you can't find tapenade, try another olive spread, or chop kalamata olives and anchovies and mix them into the tuna.

3 SERVINGS

1 tablespoon red wine vinegar

1 tablespoon extra-virgin olive oil

1 (6-ounce) can white tuna packed in water, drained

1 tomato, seeded and chopped

1/2 cup chopped fennel or 1 celery stalk, chopped

1 scallion, white and light green parts only, thinly sliced, or 1 tablespoon chopped red onion

Salt and freshly ground black pepper

3 tablespoons tapenade or other olive spread

3 whole wheat rolls, split

2 hard-boiled eggs, thinly sliced

1 cup arugula or other lettuce

In a bowl, combine the vinegar and olive oil. Add the tuna, flaking it into small pieces. Add the tomato, fennel, and scallion and stir to combine. Season lightly with salt and pepper.

Spread 1 tablespoon of tapenade on the top of each roll. Divide the eggs on the bottom of each roll. Top with the tuna mixture, arugula, and remaining half of the roll. Serve as is, or cover in plastic wrap and top with a baking sheet weighed down with cans or a heavy pot for 10 minutes, pushing down occasionally to condense the sandwich.

PER SERVING

Calories	310
Calories from fat	120
Fat	14 g
Saturated fat	3 g
Trans fatty acids, total	0 g
Polyunsaturated fat	2.5 g
Monounsaturated fat	5 g
Cholesterol	145 mg
Sodium	570 mg
Carbohydrate	27 g
Dietary fiber	5 g
Sugars	7 g
Protein	20 g

 TIP *Use leftover fennel for Chicken Paillard with Arugula and Fennel (page 66).*

CHICKEN WALDORF SALAD

It's always fun to put a spin on a traditional recipe. The classic Waldorf salad, full of chopped apple, walnuts, and celery, transforms into a more substantial meal with the addition of cooked chicken. Bake your own (page 204) or use a purchased bird.

Here, the salad is served on top of a bed of greens, but it can also be sandwiched between slices of bread for lunch or to eat on the go.

4 SERVINGS

1/4 cup "light" or reduced-fat mayonnaise

1/4 cup nonfat plain Greek yogurt

1 tablespoon fresh lemon juice

2 cups chopped cooked chicken breast

1 celery stalk, chopped

1 small apple, cored and chopped

1/4 cup raisins, golden raisins, or dried sweetened cranberries

1/4 cup chopped toasted walnuts

2 tablespoons chopped fresh Italian parsley, optional

Salt and freshly ground black pepper

8 cups mixed greens

In a bowl, combine the mayonnaise, yogurt, and lemon juice. Add the chicken, celery, apple, raisins, walnuts, and parsley, if desired, and stir to combine. Season with salt and pepper.

Serve on top of mixed greens.

PER SERVING

Calories	270
Calories from fat	100
Fat	11 g
Saturated fat	1.5 g
Trans fatty acids, total	0 g
Polyunsaturated fat	6 g
Monounsaturated fat	2.5 g
Cholesterol	60 mg
Sodium	210 mg
Carbohydrate	17 g
Dietary fiber	3 g
Sugars	11 g
Protein	26 g

 TIP *Choose a sweet but semifirm apple you like to eat on its own.*

PEARL COUSCOUS "TABBOULEH"

A lot of people think that couscous is a grain, but it is actually a type of pasta.

Here, pearl couscous, also known as Israeli couscous, is combined with the herbs and vegetables traditionally found in classic tabbouleh for an unexpected twist.

Pearl couscous has a unique toothsome texture and cooks quickly. Toasting it first in a skillet adds a slightly nutty flavor.

4 SERVINGS

1 cup pearl couscous

2 cups reduced-sodium chicken or vegetable broth

2 Roma tomatoes, seeded and chopped

1/2 cucumber, peeled, seeded, and chopped

1/2 cup chopped fresh Italian parsley

2 tablespoons finely chopped red onion

2 tablespoons chopped fresh mint

2 tablespoons extra-virgin olive oil

2 to 3 tablespoons fresh lemon juice

Salt and freshly ground black pepper

In a skillet over medium-high heat, add the couscous and sauté for 1 to 2 minutes or until lightly golden. Add the broth and bring to a boil. Reduce the heat and simmer for 6 to 8 minutes, stirring until almost all the liquid is absorbed. Cover and set aside for 5 minutes.

Meanwhile, in a bowl, combine the tomatoes, cucumber, parsley, onion, and mint. Add the couscous and stir to combine. In a bowl, combine the oil and 2 tablespoons of the lemon juice (or put into a jar and shake well). Drizzle the dressing over the couscous to lightly coat, and stir gently to combine. Season with salt and pepper and additional lemon juice, if desired.

PER SERVING	
Calories	220
Calories from fat	60
Fat	7 g
Saturated fat	1 g
Trans fatty acids, total	0 g
Polyunsaturated fat	1 g
Monounsaturated fat	5 g
Cholesterol	0 mg
Sodium	270 mg
Carbohydrate	33 g
Dietary fiber	2 g
Sugars	2 g
Protein	7 g

If you can't find ripe Roma tomatoes, use 1 cup of chopped cherry tomatoes. If you use a 6-ounce box of pearl couscous, follow the package instructions for the amount of liquid needed.

CAULIFLOWER AND LEEK SOUP

You would never guess this rich and creamy soup is, in fact, made with no cream at all. Puréed cauliflower delivers a lush and rich consistency, sure to satisfy even the hungriest eater. It's a filling vegan option when made with vegetable broth.

Top with a sprinkle of chives for added flavor.

6 SERVINGS

2 tablespoons canola oil

2 leeks, white and light green parts only, halved lengthwise and sliced

2 garlic cloves, minced

1 head (about 1$\frac{1}{2}$ pounds) cauliflower, cored and cut into 1-inch pieces

4 to 5 cups reduced-sodium chicken or vegetable broth

Salt and freshly ground black pepper

1 tablespoon thinly sliced fresh chives, optional

In a stockpot over medium heat, add the oil. Sauté the leeks for 5 to 8 minutes, or until softened. Add the garlic and sauté for 1 minute. Add the cauliflower and stir to combine. Add 4 cups of the broth (it will barely cover the cauliflower) and bring to a boil. Reduce the heat, cover, and simmer for 30 minutes, or until cauliflower is very tender, stirring occasionally.

Working in batches, transfer to a blender or food processor and let cool slightly before puréeing until smooth. Return to the stockpot over low heat and stir. If the soup is too thick, add broth. Season with salt and pepper and sprinkle with chives, if desired.

PER SERVING	
Calories	80
Calories from fat	45
Fat	5 g
Saturated fat	0.5 g
Trans fatty acids, total	0 g
Polyunsaturated fat	1.5 g
Monounsaturated fat	3 g
Cholesterol	0 mg
Sodium	360 mg
Carbohydrate	7 g
Dietary fiber	1 g
Sugars	3 g
Protein	3 g

 TIP *Leeks can have grit in their root ends. To get them really clean, slice them lengthwise to expose the interior root (where dirt hides) and rinse very well.*

NOTES

SIDE DISHES

BROCCOLI AND SHIITAKE STIR-FRY

For most people, steamed broccoli is a perfunctory addition to a meal. But with only a few minutes of effort, it can be transformed into a truly memorable side dish. The addition of shiitake mushrooms provides a contrast in textures, and the glossy sauce coats the vegetables with rich flavor.

4 SERVINGS

1 tablespoon canola oil

1 pound broccoli florets

1/4 cup water

4 ounces shiitake mushrooms, sliced

3 garlic cloves, thinly sliced

Pinch crushed red pepper flakes

2 tablespoons reduced-sodium soy sauce

2 tablespoons oyster sauce

2 tablespoons rice vinegar

1 teaspoon dark sesame oil

1 tablespoon cornstarch

In a large, preferably nonstick, skillet over medium-high heat, add the oil. Sauté the broccoli for 1 minute. Add the water, cover, and cook for 3 to 5 minutes, stirring occasionally, or until softened and bright green. Reduce the heat to medium, add the mushrooms, garlic, and red pepper flakes, and sauté for 2 minutes.

Meanwhile, in a bowl, combine the soy sauce, oyster sauce, vinegar, sesame oil, and cornstarch.

Reduce the heat to medium-low, pour the sauce over the vegetables, and bring to a simmer for 1 minute, stirring to combine.

PER SERVING

Calories	90
Calories from fat	45
Fat	5 g
Saturated fat	0.5 g
Trans fatty acids, total	0 g
Polyunsaturated fat	1.5 g
Monounsaturated fat	2.5 g
Cholesterol	0 mg
Sodium	500 mg
Carbohydrate	10 g
Dietary fiber	3 g
Sugars	3 g
Protein	4 g

For a vegetarian meal, serve with quinoa, brown rice, or another grain.

SAUTÉED BRUSSELS SPROUTS WITH JALAPEÑOS

When you need a vegetable on the table in less than five minutes, try shredded Brussels sprouts. They are delicious with just a sprinkle of salt, but in this recipe, they are given a slightly southwestern flair with the addition of chopped jalapeño and cilantro.

Serve with Chicken-Black Bean "Tamale" Casserole (page 43).

4 SERVINGS

1 pound Brussels sprouts, trimmed

1 garlic clove

1 jalapeño pepper, halved and seeded

1/4 cup fresh cilantro

1 tablespoon canola oil

Salt and freshly ground black pepper

In a food processor fitted with the thin slicing blade, shred the Brussels sprouts. Transfer to a bowl. Change to the chopping blade. With the motor running, add the garlic. Scrape down the sides, add the jalapeño and cilantro, and pulse to combine.

In a large skillet over medium-high heat, add the oil. Sauté the Brussels sprouts for 2 to 3 minutes, or until softened and bright green. Add the garlic mixture and sauté for 1 minute. Season with salt and pepper.

PER SERVING

Calories	80
Calories from fat	40
Fat	4 g
Saturated fat	0.5 g
Trans fatty acids, total	0 g
Polyunsaturated fat	1.5 g
Monounsaturated fat	2.5 g
Cholesterol	0 mg
Sodium	25 mg
Carbohydrate	9 g
Dietary fiber	3 g
Sugars	3 g
Protein	3 g

 TIP *A food processor is helpful for chopping and slicing large amounts of vegetables, but you can chop and slice by hand if you don't have one.*

CORN, AVOCADO, AND TOMATO SALAD

When corn is in season and you find yourself with a few extra ears, make them count. This salad makes a perfect accompaniment for a Mexican-style entrée like Zesty Fish Tacos with Avocado (page 47) or Portobello and Poblano Tacos (page 42) or as an appetizer served with baked tortilla chips.

Use these measurements as a guide, but feel free to tinker to your liking. If you are using fresh corn, boil or steam three ears for one minute before cutting the kernels off the cob. If you don't have fresh, use frozen (defrosted) or canned corn.

4 TO 6 SERVINGS

2 cups corn

1 cup grape tomatoes, halved

1/2 small red onion, chopped

1 jalapeño pepper, seeded and finely chopped

2 tablespoons fresh lime juice

1 tablespoon olive oil

1 teaspoon ground cumin

Salt and freshly ground black pepper

1 avocado, cut into 1/2-inch pieces

1/4 cup chopped fresh cilantro

In a bowl, combine the corn, tomatoes, onion, and jalapeño.

In a bowl, combine the lime juice, oil, and cumin (or put into a jar and shake well). Drizzle the dressing over the salad to lightly coat and stir gently to combine. Season with salt and pepper. Add avocado and cilantro and stir gently to combine.

PER SERVING	
Calories	180
Calories from fat	90
Fat	10 g
Saturated fat	1.5 g
Trans fatty acids, total	0 g
Polyunsaturated fat	1.5 g
Monounsaturated fat	7 g
Cholesterol	0 mg
Sodium	10 mg
Carbohydrate	23 g
Dietary fiber	5 g
Sugars	6 g
Protein	4 g

TIP *A good way to control "flying kernels" when cutting corn off the cob is to place the ear in a bowl with the flat end on an overturned small ramekin or glass. Cut downward carefully. The bowl will rein in any errant pieces.*

STRING BEANS WITH GINGER AND GARLIC

Turn green beans into something spectacular in about five minutes with only a few ingredients! Blanching vegetables prevents you from overcooking them so they stay crisp and retain their vibrant color. It also allows you to cook them partially ahead of time so all you have to do is quickly sauté them before serving.

4 SERVINGS

1 pound green beans, trimmed

1 tablespoon canola oil

3 garlic cloves, minced

1 (1-inch) piece peeled fresh ginger, minced

1 tablespoon reduced-sodium soy sauce

1 teaspoon dark sesame oil

Fill a large bowl with ice water.

In a stockpot of boiling water, add the string beans and cook for 2 to 3 minutes, or until just tender and bright green. Drain and transfer to ice water to cool. Drain well and pat dry.

In a large skillet over medium-high heat, add the oil. Sauté the garlic and ginger for 1 minute. Add the string beans and soy sauce and sauté for 1 minute, or until heated through. Transfer to a bowl and drizzle with sesame oil.

PER SERVING

Calories	80
Calories from fat	45
Fat	5 g
Saturated fat	0.5 g
Trans fatty acids, total	0 g
Polyunsaturated fat	1.5 g
Monounsaturated fat	2.5 g
Cholesterol	0 mg
Sodium	140 mg
Carbohydrate	9 g
Dietary fiber	3 g
Sugars	2 g
Protein	2 g

SAUTÉED SPINACH WITH RAISINS AND PINE NUTS

Enjoying spinach is easy when it's lightly sautéed so it tastes fresh and vibrant. This recipe, enhanced with garlic, pine nuts, and raisins, will further entice diners to try this vitamin-, mineral-, and carotenoids-rich vegetable.

For more flavor, soak the raisins in apple juice or white wine instead of water and drizzle the dish with extra-virgin olive oil before serving.

4 SERVINGS

1/3 cup golden raisins

1 tablespoon olive oil

2 garlic cloves, thinly sliced

1 shallot, minced

2 pounds fresh baby spinach

Salt and freshly ground black pepper

1/4 cup pine nuts, toasted

Extra-virgin olive oil, optional

In a bowl, combine the raisins and warm water for 5 to 10 minutes. Drain and pat dry.

Meanwhile, in a stockpot over medium heat, add the oil. Sauté the garlic and shallot for 1 to 2 minutes, or until softened. Add the spinach a handful at a time, stirring to incorporate and coat with oil, until just wilted and bright green. Drain any excess liquid from the pot and transfer the spinach to a bowl. Season with salt and pepper.

Top the spinach with the raisins and pine nuts and a drizzle of extra-virgin oil, if desired.

PER SERVING	
Calories	180
Calories from fat	90
Fat	10 g
Saturated fat	1 g
Trans fatty acids, total	0 g
Polyunsaturated fat	3.5 g
Monounsaturated fat	4 g
Cholesterol	0 mg
Sodium	180 mg
Carbohydrate	20 g
Dietary fiber	6 g
Sugars	9 g
Protein	8 g

TIP *When toasted, delicate pine nuts have a deep, buttery flavor. You can cook them in the oven (or toaster oven) or sauté them in a dry skillet. They go from golden to burned quickly, so watch them carefully, stir frequently, and trust your nose to sense when they are just done. Once golden, remove them to a plate to prevent further browning.*

SWEET POTATO SALAD WITH DRIED CRANBERRIES

After tasting this potato salad, you may never choose the classic version again. This sweet and savory combination is welcome at any fall picnic or meal. For more crunch, add chopped apples.

Sweet potato salad is also a great make-ahead dish for Thanksgiving. Even better, it can be served warm, chilled, or at room temperature.

4 SERVINGS

1 very large or 2 small sweet potatoes (about 1 1/2 pounds), peeled and cut into 1-inch pieces

1 tablespoon olive oil

Salt and freshly ground black pepper

1 tablespoon apple cider vinegar

1 tablespoon light brown sugar

1 teaspoon Dijon mustard

1 tablespoon extra-virgin olive oil

1/4 cup dried sweetened cranberries

2 tablespoons chopped red onion

2 tablespoons chopped fresh Italian parsley

1 celery stalk, chopped

Preheat the oven to 400 degrees.

Lightly coat a foil-lined, rimmed baking sheet with nonstick cooking spray. Place the sweet potato pieces on the baking sheet and drizzle with the olive oil. Sprinkle with salt and pepper and stir to combine. Evenly distribute the sweet potato pieces on the baking sheet. Roast for 20 to 30 minutes, or until tender and slightly charred, stirring the potatoes every 10 minutes.

Meanwhile, in a bowl, combine the vinegar, brown sugar, and mustard. Slowly whisk in the extra-virgin olive oil to incorporate (or put into a jar and shake well).

In a bowl, combine the cranberries, onion, parsley, and celery. Add the sweet potatoes and stir gently to combine. Drizzle the dressing over the salad to lightly coat and stir gently to combine. Season with salt and pepper.

PER SERVING	
Calories	200
Calories from fat	60
Fat	7 g
Saturated fat	1 g
Trans fatty acids, total	0 g
Polyunsaturated fat	1 g
Monounsaturated fat	5 g
Cholesterol	0 mg
Sodium	80 mg
Carbohydrate	33 g
Dietary fiber	4 g
Sugars	16 g
Protein	2 g

In addition to providing fiber and potassium, sweet potatoes are a vitamin A powerhouse.

POLENTA FRIES TWO WAYS

In these recipes, cooked polenta is cut into strips and broiled until crispy on the edges and golden brown. They are an unexpected but delicious substitute for French fries. You can buy cooked polenta packaged in tubes in most supermarkets, though the size of packaging may vary slightly.

PARMESAN POLENTA FRIES

Dust the "fries" with Parmesan cheese to add a hint of flavor.

5 SERVINGS

1 (18-ounce) tube polenta

1 tablespoon olive oil

2 tablespoons freshly grated Parmesan cheese

Preheat the broiler to high and set an oven rack 3 to 4 inches from the heat. Lightly coat a foil-lined, rimmed baking sheet with nonstick cooking spray.

Slice the polenta into $1/2$-inch rounds and then into $1/2$-inch "fries" (some will be slightly rounded). Place the pieces on the baking sheet and brush with oil. Broil for 5 to 6 minutes, or until golden brown. Flip, brush with oil, and sprinkle with Parmesan. Broil for 3 to 5 minutes, or until crispy on the edges and golden.

PER SERVING

Calories	100
Calories from fat	30
Fat	3.5 g
Saturated fat	0.5 g
Trans fatty acids, total	0 g
Polyunsaturated fat	0.5 g
Monounsaturated fat	2 g
Cholesterol	0 mg
Sodium	280 mg
Carbohydrate	15 g
Dietary fiber	1 g
Sugars	0 g
Protein	2 g

POLENTA FRIES WITH BLUE CHEESE DIPPING SAUCE

A simple dip made of blue cheese and nonfat yogurt makes these cornmeal sticks extra delicious.

5 SERVINGS

1 (18-ounce tube) polenta

1 tablespoon olive oil

1/4 cup crumbled blue cheese

2 tablespoons nonfat plain Greek yogurt

1 tablespoon "light" or reduced-fat mayonnaise

1 tablespoon fresh lemon juice

1 to 2 tablespoons low-fat milk

2 to 3 pinches garlic powder, or to taste

2 to 3 pinches onion powder, or to taste

1 to 2 shakes hot sauce, or to taste

Salt and freshly ground black pepper

Preheat the broiler to high and set an oven rack 3 to 4 inches from the heat. Lightly coat a foil-lined, rimmed baking sheet with nonstick cooking spray.

Slice the polenta into 1/2-inch rounds and then into 1/2-inch "fries" (some will be slightly rounded). Place the pieces on the baking sheet and brush with oil. Broil for 5 to 6 minutes, or until golden brown. Flip and brush with oil. Broil for 3 to 5 minutes, or until crispy on the edges and golden.

Meanwhile, in a bowl, combine the blue cheese, yogurt, mayonnaise, lemon juice, 1 tablespoon milk, garlic powder, onion powder, and hot sauce. Season with salt and pepper and additional garlic powder, onion powder, or hot sauce, if desired. If the sauce is too thick, add milk.

PER SERVING

Calories	130
Calories from fat	50
Fat	6 g
Saturated fat	2 g
Trans fatty acids, total	0 g
Polyunsaturated fat	1 g
Monounsaturated fat	3 g
Cholesterol	5 mg
Sodium	370 mg
Carbohydrate	16 g
Dietary fiber	1 g
Sugars	1 g
Protein	4 g

HONEY-ROASTED CARROTS, PARSNIPS, AND DATES

In this scrumptious side, a light sauce infuses roasted carrots and parsnips with flavor and subtle aroma, and dates provide added texture. Serve as is or over quinoa, brown rice, or another whole grain for a vegetarian dinner or lunch.

At first there might seem to be more liquid than necessary, but it will thicken and coat the vegetables as they cook, especially if the baking sheet is on a lower oven rack. As you stir the vegetables, you can judge how quickly they're cooking and move them from the lower rack to the middle or vice versa.

If you only have one type of citrus, juice the whole fruit.

6 SERVINGS

Juice of 1/2 lemon

Juice of 1/2 orange

2 tablespoons honey

1 tablespoon olive oil

2 teaspoons whole grain mustard

1 pound carrots, cut into 1-inch pieces

1 pound parsnips, cut into 1-inch pieces

8 pitted dates, halved

Salt and freshly ground black pepper

Preheat the oven to 400 degrees.

Lightly coat a foil-lined, rimmed baking sheet with nonstick cooking spray.

In a bowl, combine the lemon juice, orange juice, honey, oil, and mustard.

In a bowl, combine the carrots, parsnips, and dates. Add the sauce and stir to combine. Evenly distribute the mixture on the baking sheet. Sprinkle with salt and pepper. Roast for 20 to 30 minutes, or until tender and slightly charred, stirring the vegetables every 10 minutes.

PER SERVING	
Calories	150
Calories from fat	25
Fat	3 g
Saturated fat	0.5 g
Trans fatty acids, total	0 g
Polyunsaturated fat	0.5 g
Monounsaturated fat	2 g
Cholesterol	0 mg
Sodium	78 mg
Carbohydrate	31 g
Dietary fiber	5 g
Sugars	19 g
Protein	2 g

TIP *Parsnips are irregularly shaped, with a thicker top and long thin bottom. To ensure even cooking, halve or quarter the thicker tops before slicing to make more uniform pieces and leave the thinner ends longer so they won't cook too quickly.*

CHICKPEAS IN SPICY TOMATO SAUCE

When you need to make a side dish and are limited to basics you likely have on hand already, try this aromatic and piquant combination. Canned chickpeas are cooked in a tomato sauce flavored with fresh ginger, cumin, and turmeric with a touch of cayenne heat. If you have fresh parsley or cilantro on hand, chop one-quarter cup and sprinkle on top after cooking.

6 SERVINGS

1 tablespoon canola oil

½ onion, finely chopped

1 (½-inch) piece peeled fresh ginger, minced

2 garlic cloves, minced

1 teaspoon ground cumin

1 teaspoon ground turmeric

⅛ teaspoon cayenne pepper

1 (14.5-ounce) can diced tomatoes

2 (15-ounce) cans chickpeas, rinsed and drained

Salt

In a large skillet over medium heat, add the oil. Sauté the onion and ginger for 3 to 5 minutes, or until softened. Add the garlic and sauté for 1 minute. Add the cumin, turmeric, and cayenne pepper and sauté for 1 minute. Add the tomatoes and their juice and bring to a boil. Reduce the heat and simmer for 10 minutes, or until thickened, stirring occasionally.

Transfer to a blender or food processor and purée until smooth. Return the sauce to the skillet, add the chickpeas, and stir to combine. Simmer for 10 minutes. Season with salt.

PER SERVING	
Calories	180
Calories from fat	40
Fat	5 g
Saturated fat	0.5 g
Trans fatty acids, total	0 g
Polyunsaturated fat	1.5 g
Monounsaturated fat	2 g
Cholesterol	0 mg
Sodium	240 mg
Carbohydrate	28 g
Dietary fiber	7 g
Sugars	7 g
Protein	8 g

ROASTED BRUSSELS SPROUTS

Who would have thought that this miniature cabbage-like vegetable would be the darling of the restaurant set? There are so many delicious ways to prepare this cruciferous vegetable, and roasting leads the way. It doesn't get much easier than this tasty side.

4 SERVINGS

1 pound Brussels sprouts, trimmed and halved lengthwise

1 tablespoon olive oil

Salt and freshly ground black pepper

Preheat the oven to 400 degrees.

Lightly coat a foil-lined, rimmed baking sheet with nonstick cooking spray. Place the Brussels sprouts on the baking sheet and drizzle with the oil. Sprinkle with salt and pepper and stir to combine. Evenly distribute the sprouts on the baking sheet. Roast for 15 to 20 minutes, or until tender and slightly charred, stirring the sprouts after 10 minutes.

PER SERVING

Calories	70
Calories from fat	35
Fat	4 g
Saturated fat	0.5 g
Trans fatty acids, total	0 g
Polyunsaturated fat	0.5 g
Monounsaturated fat	2.5 g
Cholesterol	0 mg
Sodium	25 mg
Carbohydrate	8 g
Dietary fiber	3 g
Sugars	2 g
Protein	3 g

 Not only high in fiber, Brussels sprouts are an excellent source of vitamins A, B6, C, and K.

HONEY COLESLAW

Instead of the typical mayonnaise topping, this has a refreshing dressing of apple cider vinegar and olive oil, which doesn't weigh the mixture down. A touch of honey lends sweetness, tempering the cabbage.

This light coleslaw is just as good as a side dish or as a sandwich topping (it goes great with the Barbecue Chicken Sandwich on page 103).

For more color, use additional shredded carrots or a sprinkling of fresh parsley.

4 SERVINGS

4 cups (7 ounces) coleslaw mix

1 teaspoon celery seed

2 tablespoons apple cider vinegar

1 tablespoon honey

2 tablespoons extra-virgin olive oil

Salt and freshly ground black pepper

In a bowl, combine the coleslaw mix and celery seed.

In a bowl, combine the vinegar and honey. Slowly whisk in the oil to incorporate (or put into a jar and shake well). Drizzle the dressing over the coleslaw mix and stir well to combine. Season with salt and pepper.

PER SERVING	
Calories	90
Calories from fat	60
Fat	7 g
Saturated fat	1 g
Trans fatty acids, total	0 g
Polyunsaturated fat	1 g
Monounsaturated fat	5 g
Cholesterol	0 mg
Sodium	15 mg
Carbohydrate	8 g
Dietary fiber	1 g
Sugars	5 g
Protein	0 g

 TIP *Keep empty small spice jars to mix small amounts of dressing.*

CARROT AND BEET SALAD

A plain carrot salad is easy to throw together when you are down to the wire and don't have much left in your produce drawer. But why not elevate it to something special by adding a raw beet for sweetness and crunch? Yes, you can eat beets raw!

Instead of the traditional combination of mayonnaise and raisins, which can be a little cloying, top the salad with a light lemon vinaigrette and sprinkle of chives for vibrancy.

Because this salad highlights the carrot flavor, freshly grate your own carrots with a food processor, mandoline, or grater instead of using preshredded carrots. Use the food processor to shred the beets, as well.

4 SERVINGS

4 carrots, shredded

1 beet, peeled, shredded, and patted dry

1 1/2 tablespoons fresh lemon juice

1/2 teaspoon granulated sugar

1/4 teaspoon Dijon mustard

1 1/2 tablespoons extra-virgin olive oil

Salt and freshly ground black pepper

1 tablespoon thinly sliced chives, optional

In a bowl, combine the carrots and beet.

In a bowl, combine the lemon juice, sugar, and mustard. Slowly whisk in the oil to incorporate (or put into a jar and shake well). Drizzle the dressing over the carrot mixture and stir well to combine. Season with salt and pepper and sprinkle with chives, if desired.

PER SERVING

Calories	80
Calories from fat	50
Fat	5 g
Saturated fat	1 g
Trans fatty acids, total	0 g
Polyunsaturated fat	0.5 g
Monounsaturated fat	3.5 g
Cholesterol	0 mg
Sodium	65 mg
Carbohydrate	9 g
Dietary fiber	2 g
Sugars	5 g
Protein	1 g

TIP *It's not necessary to peel the carrots before using; just rinse them well. Use caution when working with beets because their juice can temporarily stain your hands or clothing.*

ROASTED CAULIFLOWER TWO WAYS

Roasting cauliflower brings out a delicious caramelized flavor that can convert even the most ardent vegetable hater. Here are two preparations that take this humble vegetable to the next level: one with a touch of sweetness from aromatic seasonings and golden raisins, the other roasted with garlic and Parmesan cheese for more savory flavor.

ROASTED CAULIFLOWER WITH RAISINS AND PINE NUTS

A combination of spices, including cumin, cinnamon, and ginger, transforms cauliflower into a distinctive side dish. Sweet raisins and buttery pine nuts add texture and flavor. Transfer the cooked mixture back to the mixing bowl to incorporate any spices still in the bowl.

4 SERVINGS

2 tablespoons olive oil

1/2 teaspoon salt

1/4 teaspoon ground cumin

1/4 teaspoon ground cinnamon

1/4 teaspoon ground ginger

1 head (about 1 1/2 pounds) cauliflower, cored and cut into 1-inch florets

1/4 cup golden raisins

2 tablespoons finely chopped fresh Italian parsley

Juice of 1/2 lemon

2 tablespoons toasted pine nuts

Preheat the oven to 400 degrees.

Lightly coat a foil-lined, rimmed baking sheet with nonstick cooking spray.

In a bowl, combine the olive oil, salt, cumin, cinnamon, and ginger. Add the cauliflower and stir to combine. Evenly distribute the cauliflower on the baking sheet. Roast for 20 to 30 minutes, or until tender and slightly charred, stirring the cauliflower every 10 minutes. Return to the bowl and add the raisins, parsley, and lemon juice and stir gently to combine. Top with the pine nuts.

PER SERVING

Calories	140
Calories from fat	90
Fat	10 g
Saturated fat	1 g
Trans fatty acids, total	0 g
Polyunsaturated fat	2 g
Monounsaturated fat	6 g
Cholesterol	0 mg
Sodium	310 mg
Carbohydrate	12 g
Dietary fiber	2 g
Sugars	7 g
Protein	2 g

ROASTED CAULIFLOWER WITH PARMESAN AND THYME

This simple preparation shows just how much cooking with high heat can bring out the best in food. You can also make this with broccoli: just omit the thyme and sprinkle with lemon zest before roasting.

4 SERVINGS

1 head (about 1 $^1/_2$ pounds) cauliflower, cored and cut into 1-inch florets

4 sprigs fresh thyme

2 tablespoons olive oil

Salt and freshly ground black pepper

5 garlic cloves, halved

2 tablespoons freshly grated Parmesan cheese

Preheat the oven to 400 degrees.

Lightly coat a foil-lined, rimmed baking sheet with nonstick cooking spray. Place the cauliflower and thyme on the baking sheet and drizzle with the oil. Sprinkle with salt and pepper and stir to combine. Evenly distribute the cauliflower on the baking sheet. Roast for 10 minutes, add the garlic, and stir to combine. Roast for 10 minutes, stir, and sprinkle with the cheese. Roast for 2 to 3 minutes, or until tender and slightly charred. Discard the thyme sprigs before serving.

PER SERVING	
Calories	90
Calories from fat	70 g
Fat	8 g
Saturated fat	1.3 g
Trans fatty acids, total	0.0 g
Polyunsaturated fat	0.7 g
Monounsaturated fat	5.1 g
Cholesterol	Less than 5 mg
Sodium	55 mg
Carbohydrate	5 g
Dietary fiber	1 g
Sugars	1 g
Protein	2 g

TIP *Use leftover thyme in Easy One-Pot Chicken and Vegetables (page 91) or Lick-the-Bowl-Good Mushroom Soup (page 97).*

MINI TWICE-BAKED POTATOES

So much of adopting healthy eating habits involves using portion control, not giving up favorite foods altogether. This version of twice-baked potatoes provides the satisfaction of the creamy treat, but using a smaller potato guarantees moderation.

Use caution when scooping out the flesh of the potato so the skin retains a "shell" to refill with the seasoned mashed potatoes. A small spoon, melon baller, or serrated grapefruit spoon would all work well for this task.

4 SERVINGS

4 (2-inch) red or yellow potatoes, halved

1 teaspoon olive oil

2 tablespoons regular or reduced-fat sour cream or nonfat plain Greek yogurt

2 tablespoons low-fat milk or buttermilk

2 tablespoons freshly grated Parmesan cheese

2 teaspoons thinly sliced fresh chives, optional

Salt and freshly ground black pepper

Preheat the oven to 425 degrees.

Lightly coat a foil-lined, rimmed baking sheet with nonstick cooking spray.

Slice a thin strip off the bottom of each potato half so it lays flat. Place the potatoes on the baking sheet and brush with oil. Bake for 25 to 35 minutes, or until very tender when pierced with a fork or skewer. Remove from the oven and set aside until cool enough to handle (but still warm). Increase the oven temperature to 450 degrees.

With a small spoon, carefully scoop out the potatoes' insides into a mixing bowl, leaving a 1/4-inch shell of potato, using care not to break the skins. To the potato flesh, add the sour cream, milk, Parmesan, and chives, if desired, and mash until creamy. Season with salt and pepper. Divide the mixture evenly among the potato shells.

Return the stuffed potatoes to the baking sheet. Bake for 8 to 10 minutes, or until the potatoes are heated through and lightly golden.

PER SERVING	
Calories	160
Calories from fat	30
Fat	3 g
Saturated fat	1.5 g
Trans fatty acids, total	0 g
Polyunsaturated fat	0 g
Monounsaturated fat	1.5 g
Cholesterol	5 mg
Sodium	60 mg
Carbohydrate	28 g
Dietary fiber	3 g
Sugars	2 g
Protein	5 g

Feel free to substitute Cheddar or another type of cheese for the Parmesan. Mix in leftover cooked chopped broccoli, sautéed mushrooms, or spinach for something more substantial.

SAUTÉED BROCCOLI RABE WITH GARLIC

Broccoli rabe, or rapini, is an assertive green that's a mainstay of Italian cooking. It's often paired with pasta, polenta, or sausage. Blanching—quick cooking followed by an ice water bath—preserves its beautiful color and eliminates some of its bitterness.

4 SERVINGS

2 pounds broccoli rabe, heavy stems removed, cut into 1-inch pieces

1 tablespoon olive oil

3 garlic cloves, thinly sliced

1/2 teaspoon crushed red pepper flakes, or to taste

1 tablespoon extra-virgin olive oil

Salt and freshly ground black pepper

Fill a large bowl with ice water.

In a stockpot of boiling water, add the broccoli rabe and cook for 1 to 2 minutes, or until just tender and bright green. Drain and transfer to ice water to cool. Drain well and pat dry.

In a large skillet over medium heat, add the olive oil. Sauté the garlic and red pepper flakes for 1 minute. Add the broccoli rabe and sauté for 1 minute, or until heated through.

Transfer to a bowl and drizzle with the extra-virgin olive oil. Season with salt and pepper and additional red pepper flakes, if desired.

PER SERVING

Calories	110
Calories from fat	70
Fat	8 g
Saturated fat	1 g
Trans fatty acids, total	0 g
Polyunsaturated fat	1 g
Monounsaturated fat	5 g
Cholesterol	0 mg
Sodium	70 mg
Carbohydrate	7 g
Dietary fiber	6 g
Sugars	1 g
Protein	7 g

For a super-fast vegetarian main course, add chickpeas and golden raisins and serve over brown rice or polenta.

SWEET AND SOUR CUCUMBER SALAD

Side dishes don't have to be fancy; they just need to be flavorful, and this one certainly is. The key when making cucumber salads is to draw out the vegetable's excess moisture by sprinkling the slices with salt, so the dressing doesn't get diluted. Pat the cucumbers completely dry before adding the dressing.

For a nicer presentation, partially peel the cukes, leaving some stripes of deep green skin to contrast with the paler flesh. Use a mandoline or food processor to get the cucumber and onion slices thin and even.

4 SERVINGS

2 large cucumbers, preferably thin-skinned seedless, very thinly sliced

1/2 small red onion, very thinly sliced

Salt

1/4 cup white vinegar or rice vinegar

1 tablespoon granulated sugar

1/2 teaspoon crushed red pepper flakes

In a colander, combine the cucumber and onion. Sprinkle with salt and set in the sink to drain for at least 15 minutes and up to an hour. Rinse well and pat dry.

Meanwhile, in a saucepan over medium heat, cook the vinegar and sugar until the sugar dissolves. Set aside to cool.

In a bowl, combine the cucumber mixture, vinegar, and red pepper flakes.

PER SERVING

Calories	50
Calories from fat	0
Fat	0 g
Saturated fat	0 g
Trans fatty acids, total	0 g
Polyunsaturated fat	0 g
Monounsaturated fat	0 g
Cholesterol	0 mg
Sodium	105 mg
Carbohydrate	12 g
Dietary fiber	1 g
Sugars	7 g
Protein	2 g

For more flavor, add a drizzle of sesame oil or a sprinkling of chopped cilantro or parsley before serving. If you don't like heat, omit the red pepper flakes.

BREAKFAST

ARTICHOKE AND GOAT CHEESE "CRUSTLESS" QUICHE

This quiche saves time and calories by dispensing with the pastry exterior. Canned artichokes, fresh dill, and goat cheese ensure it comes together quickly without sacrificing flavor. You can substitute any of your favorite ingredients.

Quiche often releases some liquid after cooking, which the crust normally absorbs. If this happens after you cut out the first piece, use a paper towel to blot the baking dish. Make sure to drain and dry the artichokes well to prevent excess weeping. If you do include other ingredients, choose ones with low water content.

6 SERVINGS

5 eggs

2 cups low-fat milk

1/2 teaspoon salt

1/4 teaspoon freshly ground black pepper

1 (14-ounce) can artichoke hearts, drained, chopped, and dried well

2 tablespoons chopped fresh dill

1 cup (4 ounces) crumbled goat cheese

Preheat the oven to 375 degrees.

Coat a 10-inch pie plate or quiche dish with nonstick cooking spray.

In a bowl, beat the eggs. Add the milk, salt, and pepper. Add the artichokes, dill, and goat cheese and stir gently to combine. Pour into the baking dish.

Bake for 45 to 55 minutes, or until the eggs are set and the center doesn't jiggle. Let rest for 10 minutes before serving.

PER SERVING	
Calories	170
Calories from fat	80
Fat	9 g
Saturated fat	4.5 g
Trans fatty acids, total	0 g
Polyunsaturated fat	1 g
Monounsaturated fat	2.5 g
Cholesterol	180 mg
Sodium	470 mg
Carbohydrate	10 g
Dietary fiber	2 g
Sugars	5 g
Protein	13 g

 TIP *Quiche is a convenient bake-and-take lunch! Leftovers are great heated or served at room temperature, plain or in a sandwich.*

MINI SPINACH AND MUSHROOM FRITTATAS

If portion control is difficult for you, these individually sized frittatas can help. Customize them by using your favorite vegetables or use up what you have in your crisper drawer.

For convenience, keep extras in the refrigerator for easy breakfasts, lunches, or snacks. Simply reheat them in the microwave for twelve to fifteen seconds.

Spray the muffin tins generously to help the frittatas come out easily after cooking. Place one-quarter cup of water in the empty cups to prevent scorching.

9 SERVINGS

2 teaspoons canola oil

4 ounces white mushrooms, coarsely chopped

2 scallions, white and light green parts only, thinly sliced

1 (5- or 6-ounce) package baby spinach

6 eggs

1/2 cup shredded Cheddar or mozzarella cheese

1/4 cup low-fat milk

Salt and freshly ground black pepper

Preheat the oven to 350 degrees.

Generously coat nine cups in a muffin tin with nonstick cooking spray.

In a small, preferably nonstick, skillet over medium-high heat, add the oil. Sauté the mushrooms and scallions for 2 to 3 minutes, or until softened. Add the spinach a handful at a time and sauté for 1 to 2 minutes, or until completely wilted. Transfer to a cutting board and coarsely chop.

Meanwhile, in a bowl, beat the eggs. Add the cheese, milk, and spinach mixture. Sprinkle generously with salt and pepper and stir well to combine. Spoon the mixture evenly into the prepared muffin cups. Bake for 13 to 15 minutes, or until just set. Leave in the tin for 1 minute before removing. Run a knife or offset spatula around the edges to release the frittatas.

PER SERVING

Calories	90
Calories from fat	60
Fat	6 g
Saturated fat	2.5 g
Trans fatty acids, total	0 g
Polyunsaturated fat	1 g
Monounsaturated fat	2.5 g
Cholesterol	130 mg
Sodium	100 mg
Carbohydrate	2 g
Dietary fiber	1 g
Sugars	1 g
Protein	7 g

Eggs are a good source of protein and vitamins A, B12, and D and have only 75 calories. One large egg contains 5 grams of total fat, of which only 1.6 grams are saturated.

EGG, PESTO, AND SUN-DRIED TOMATO WRAP

If you are trying to limit your fat intake, egg whites are a great choice for breakfast. But don't malign the whole egg. Recent research indicates that dietary cholesterol isn't the biggest determinant of overall cholesterol levels for many people. So even if you are being very careful, adding a yolk won't be a problem.

1 SERVING

- 1 teaspoon olive oil
- 1 cup fresh baby spinach
- 2 sun-dried tomatoes packed in oil, patted dry
- 2 egg whites, beaten
- ½ teaspoon pesto
- 1 (5- to 6-inch) whole wheat, flour, or corn tortilla
- 1 tablespoon shredded mozzarella cheese

In an 8- or 10-inch nonstick skillet over medium-high heat, add the oil. Sauté the spinach for 1 to 2 minutes, or until completely wilted. Transfer to a cutting board, add the sun-dried tomatoes, and coarsely chop.

In the same skillet, over medium heat, add the egg whites and cook without stirring for 30 to 45 seconds, or until the eggs are set on the bottom. Using a spatula, lift the edges of the egg whites toward the center of the skillet and gently tilt the pan so the uncooked eggs run underneath the bottom until the eggs are cooked through. Top half of the egg whites with the spinach mixture and fold over the other half, pressing to seal. Transfer to a plate.

Spread the pesto on the tortilla and sprinkle with cheese. Place the tortilla, cheese side up, in the skillet and cook for 30 seconds, or until the cheese begins to melt. Place the egg on half of the tortilla (folding it to fit if necessary), fold the tortilla over it to eat like a taco, and cook for 20 to 30 seconds.

PER SERVING

Calories	230
Calories from fat	110
Fat	12 g
Saturated fat	3.5 g
Trans fatty acids, total	0 g
Polyunsaturated fat	1.5 g
Monounsaturated fat	7 g
Cholesterol	5 mg
Sodium	440 mg
Carbohydrate	17 g
Dietary fiber	5 g
Sugars	2 g
Protein	14 g

 You can skip the tortilla and have this as an egg white omelet if you prefer: just spread the pesto and cheese on half of the omelet before folding.

PUMPKIN AND DOUBLE-GINGER MUFFINS

These muffins bring the autumnal flavors of pumpkins and cranberries to mornings all year long. Using both ground and crystallized ginger adds punch, and canned pumpkin purée keeps them moist and boosts antioxidants and vitamins.

12 MUFFINS

1 cup all-purpose flour

1/2 cup whole wheat flour

1/2 cup granulated sugar

1/4 cup light brown sugar

1 teaspoon baking soda

1 teaspoon ground ginger

1/2 teaspoon ground cinnamon

1/4 teaspoon baking powder

1/4 teaspoon salt

Pinch ground nutmeg

1 cup dried sweetened cranberries

2 tablespoons finely chopped crystallized ginger

1 egg

1/4 cup canola oil

1/2 cup low-fat buttermilk

1 cup canned pumpkin

Preheat the oven to 375 degrees.

Coat a muffin tin with nonstick cooking spray or fill with liners.

In a bowl, combine both flours, both sugars, baking soda, ginger, cinnamon, baking powder, salt, and nutmeg. Add the cranberries and crystallized ginger and stir to coat with the flour.

In a bowl, beat the egg. Add the oil, buttermilk, and pumpkin and stir to combine. Add to the flour mixture and stir gently until just combined. Spoon the batter evenly into the muffin cups.

Bake for 20 to 25 minutes, or until the tops just bounce back when touched. Leave in the tin for 5 to 10 minutes before removing the muffins to a cooling rack.

PER SERVING (one muffin)

Calories	180
Calories from fat	50
Fat	5 g
Saturated fat	0.5 g
Trans fatty acids, total	0 g
Polyunsaturated fat	1.5 g
Monounsaturated fat	3 g
Cholesterol	15 mg
Sodium	180 mg
Carbohydrate	32 g
Dietary fiber	2 g
Sugars	20 g
Protein	2 g

CRANBERRY, ORANGE, AND GINGER COMPOTE

Serve this compote, a mixture of lightly cooked fresh and dried fruit, as a surprising addition to a breakfast buffet. The combination of fresh cranberries and oranges fills a void when fresh berries are out of season.

Eat the compote on its own or mix it into oatmeal or yogurt. The mixture might thicken as it stands. If necessary, add juice to thin it out.

Section the oranges over a bowl or cutting board to catch their juice. If you have a pomegranate, add one-quarter cup of seeds with the oranges for texture.

4 TO 6 SERVINGS

2 cups fresh cranberries

3/4 cup fresh or high-quality store-bought orange juice

1/4 cup granulated sugar

1/4 cup chopped dried apricots or golden raisins

2 tablespoons chopped crystallized ginger

2 oranges, peel and pith removed, sectioned, and cut into 1-inch pieces

1/4 cup pomegranate seeds, optional

In a saucepan over medium-high heat, simmer the cranberries, orange juice, sugar, apricots, and ginger for 5 to 10 minutes, or until the cranberries just start to split and the mixture thickens. Remove from heat and add the orange sections and any accumulated juices and pomegranate seeds, if desired. Stir to combine.

PER SERVING

Calories	170
Calories from fat	0
Fat	0.5 g
Saturated fat	0 g
Trans fatty acids, total	0 g
Polyunsaturated fat	0 g
Monounsaturated fat	0 g
Cholesterol	0 mg
Sodium	2 mg
Carbohydrate	43 g
Dietary fiber	5 g
Sugars	35 g
Protein	2 g

TIP *An easy way to prep the oranges is to cut off the peel at the bottom so the orange stands upright. Using a sharp paring knife and following the shape of the orange, cut away the peel and pith as close to the flesh as possible. Working over a bowl to catch the juice, remove the flesh of the orange from the segments and cut into bite-sized pieces.*

CHAI OATMEAL

The flavors in chai tea—cardamom, cloves, and cinnamon—are so warming it seems only natural to pair them with oatmeal, the ultimate comforting cold-weather breakfast. Gently steeping the spices in milk adds just enough flavor without being overwhelming. The addition of brown sugar provides a hint of sweetness. Top with chopped pears and raisins or apples and dates for even more yumminess.

2 SERVINGS

2 cups low-fat milk

6 cardamom pods

5 whole cloves

4 black peppercorns

1 cinnamon stick

1/4 teaspoon vanilla extract

2 tablespoons light brown sugar

1 cup quick-cooking (not instant) oats

1/8 teaspoon salt

In a saucepan over medium-low heat, combine the milk, cardamom, cloves, peppercorns, cinnamon stick, and vanilla. Simmer for 5 minutes, swirling the pan frequently. Strain and discard the solids. Return the milk to the saucepan, add the sugar, and simmer until the sugar dissolves. Add the oats and salt and simmer for 4 to 7 minutes, or until it reaches the desired consistency, stirring occasionally.

PER SERVING	
Calories	310
Calories from fat	45
Fat	5 g
Saturated fat	2 g
Trans fatty acids, total	0 g
Polyunsaturated fat	1 g
Monounsaturated fat	1.5 g
Cholesterol	10 mg
Sodium	260 mg
Carbohydrate	53 g
Dietary fiber	4 g
Sugars	27 g
Protein	14 g

TIP *Look for whole spices in health food stores or specialty markets. For superior flavor, you can pulverize them in a coffee grinder to use in recipes that call for ground spices.*

SOUTHWEST TOFU SCRAMBLE

For a vegan breakfast option, try substituting tofu for eggs. Add a little turmeric with the spices for a yellow egg-like color. Because tofu is a perfect "sponge" for absorbing the flavors it's cooked with, don't be afraid to be liberal with spices and other veggies.

6 SERVINGS

1 (14-ounce) package firm tofu, drained

1 tablespoon canola oil

1/2 red onion, chopped

1/2 red bell pepper, seeded and chopped

1/2 green bell pepper, seeded and chopped

1 jalapeño pepper, seeded and finely chopped

1 tomato, seeded and chopped

1/4 teaspoon ground cumin

1/4 teaspoon chili powder

1/4 cup chopped fresh cilantro

Salt and freshly ground black pepper

Hot sauce, optional

Line a plate with paper towels and place the tofu on top. Cover with paper towels and top with another plate and push down to release some of its water. Set aside for 5 minutes, pushing occasionally and changing the paper towels if necessary. Using a potato masher or fork, break up the tofu into small pieces.

In a large skillet over medium heat, add the oil. Sauté the onion for 3 to 5 minutes. Add bell peppers and jalapeño and sauté for 3 minutes, or until softened. Add the tomato, cumin, and chili powder and stir well to combine.

Move the vegetables to the side and add the tofu and sauté for 2 minutes. Add the cilantro and stir to combine with the other vegetables. Season with salt and pepper and hot sauce, if desired.

PER SERVING

Calories	90
Calories from fat	50
Fat	5 g
Saturated fat	1 g
Trans fatty acids, total	0 g
Polyunsaturated fat	2 g
Monounsaturated fat	2.5 g
Cholesterol	0 mg
Sodium	12 mg
Carbohydrate	5 g
Dietary fiber	2 g
Sugars	3 g
Protein	6 g

KITCHEN SINK FRITTATA

When you find yourself with a ragtag collection of leftover veggies, one easy way to use them up is to sauté them and mix into a frittata.

Make sure you use a nonstick skillet so you can easily transfer the cooked frittata. If it's an older skillet and the finish is not as "nonstick" as it once was, remove the vegetables after sautéing and coat the skillet with nonstick cooking spray before returning them and adding the eggs.

4 TO 6 SERVINGS

1 tablespoon olive oil

1 small new potato, shredded and squeezed dry

3 white or other mushrooms, chopped

1/2 small zucchini, shredded and squeezed dry

1/2 red bell pepper, seeded and chopped

1 cup fresh baby spinach

2 tablespoons finely chopped red onion

4 eggs plus 4 egg whites

1/2 teaspoon salt

Pinch freshly ground black pepper

1 cup (2 ounces) Asiago, Manchego, or other sharp hard cheese, shaved

Preheat the oven to 350 degrees.

In a 10- or 11-inch nonstick, ovenproof skillet over medium-high heat, add the oil. Sauté the potatoes for 3 to 5 minutes, or until golden brown. Add the mushrooms, zucchini, bell pepper, spinach, and onion and sauté for 3 to 5 minutes, or until softened.

Meanwhile, in a bowl, beat the eggs, egg whites, salt, and pepper.

Reduce the heat to medium and pour the eggs on top of the vegetables. Cook without stirring for 1 minute, or until the eggs are set on the bottom. Using a spatula, lift the edges of the frittata toward the center of the skillet and gently tilt the pan so the uncooked eggs run underneath the bottom of the frittata. Cook for 20 to 30 seconds and repeat the process several times until the egg on top is wet, but not runny.

Transfer to the oven and bake for 2 to 3 minutes, or until the top is just set. Top with the cheese. Bake for 1 to 2 minutes or until the cheese melts. Do not overcook. Remove the pan from the oven and run a spatula around the skillet edge to loosen the frittata. Serve from the pan or slide or invert it onto a serving plate.

PER SERVING	
Calories	200
Calories from fat	120
Fat	13 g
Saturated fat	5 g
Trans fatty acids, total	0 g
Polyunsaturated fat	1.5 g
Monounsaturated fat	5 g
Cholesterol	200 mg
Sodium	580 mg
Carbohydrate	7 g
Dietary fiber	1 g
Sugars	2 g
Protein	15 g

TIP *Frittatas can be served for breakfast, lunch, or dinner. They can be eaten hot, at room temperature, or chilled, on their own or sandwiched between bread.*

SOFT-BOILED EGGS ON TOAST TWO WAYS

Soft-boiled eggs get a boost of healthy fats when layered with a vegetarian spread of your choice.

For many cooks, soft-boiling eggs is less intimidating than poaching but with similar results: a cooked white and softer yolk. There are almost as many variations on how to boil eggs as there are cookbooks, but in this recipe the eggs are gently simmered to keep both the white and yolk tender. You can substitute a poached or fried egg, if you prefer.

SOFT-BOILED EGGS WITH AVOCADO AND HOT SAUCE

This is a protein-packed breakfast or lunch. The winning combination of protein-filled eggs, avocado (a source of monounsaturated, or "good," fat), and whole grain bread will keep you full for longer.

1 TO 2 SERVINGS

2 eggs

1/4 avocado

2 slices whole wheat or other 100 percent whole grain bread, lightly toasted

Sriracha or other hot sauce

Salt and freshly ground black pepper

In a saucepan, bring 4 to 5 inches of water to a boil. Reduce the heat, add the eggs, and simmer for 6 minutes for a medium-runny yolk or 7 minutes for a slightly firm yolk.

Meanwhile, in a bowl, lightly mash the avocado. Season with salt and pepper. Divide the avocado on the toast and dot with Sriracha.

Run the eggs under cold water until cool enough to peel. Slice the egg over the toast. Season with salt and pepper.

PER SERVING	
Calories	340
Calories from fat	150
Fat	17 g
Saturated fat	4.5 g
Trans fatty acids, total	0 g
Polyunsaturated fat	3.5 g
Monounsaturated fat	8 g
Cholesterol	370 mg
Sodium	400 mg
Carbohydrate	28 g
Dietary fiber	6 g
Sugars	3 g
Protein	20 g

SOFT-BOILED EGGS WITH HUMMUS AND HOT SAUCE

Hummus is another heart-healthy way to get protein and good fat. It goes surprisingly well with eggs!

1 TO 2 SERVINGS

2 eggs

2 tablespoons hummus

2 slices whole wheat or other 100 percent whole grain bread, lightly toasted

Sriracha or other hot sauce

Salt and freshly ground black pepper

In a saucepan, bring 4 to 5 inches of water to a boil. Reduce the heat, add the eggs, and simmer for 6 minutes for a medium-runny yolk or 7 minutes for a slightly firm yolk.

Divide the hummus on the toast and dot with Sriracha.

Run the eggs under cold water until cool enough to peel. Slice the egg over the toast. Season with salt and pepper.

PER SERVING

Calories	330
Calories from fat	130
Fat	14 g
Saturated fat	4 g
Trans fatty acids, total	0 g
Polyunsaturated fat	4 g
Monounsaturated fat	5 g
Cholesterol	370 mg
Sodium	500 mg
Carbohydrate	29 g
Dietary fiber	5 g
Sugars	4 g
Protein	22 g

 TIP *Consuming raw or undercooked eggs can increase your risk of foodborne illness. When serving an egg with a runny center, use the freshest eggs you can find or use pasteurized eggs. You can also simmer for another minute for a totally cooked yolk.*

OATMEAL-RAISIN MUFFINS

These hearty, filling muffins, scented with cinnamon and cloves, have the taste of an oatmeal-raisin cookie but will tide you over til lunchtime.

The oatmeal needs time to soften, so start soaking it before you preheat the oven to give it a few extra minutes. Coating the raisins with flour helps keep them from sinking to the bottom of the muffins.

12 MUFFINS

1 cup old-fashioned rolled oats

1 cup low-fat buttermilk

1 cup all-purpose flour

1 teaspoon baking powder

1/2 teaspoon ground cinnamon

1/2 teaspoon baking soda

1/4 teaspoon ground cloves

1/4 teaspoon salt

1/2 cup raisins

2 eggs

1/2 cup packed light brown sugar

1/3 cup canola oil

In a bowl, combine the oats and buttermilk. Set aside for 15 minutes.

Preheat the oven to 400 degrees.

Coat a muffin tin with nonstick cooking spray or fill with liners.

In a bowl, combine the flour, baking powder, cinnamon, baking soda, cloves, and salt. Add the raisins and stir to coat with flour.

In a bowl, beat the eggs. Add the brown sugar and oil and stir to combine. Add the oat mixture, stirring well to combine. Add to the flour mixture and stir gently until just combined. Spoon the batter evenly into the muffin cups.

Bake for 13 to 18 minutes, or until the tops just bounce back when touched. Leave in the tin for 5 to 10 minutes before removing the muffins to a cooling rack.

PER SERVING (one muffin)	
Calories	190
Calories from fat	70
Fat	8 g
Saturated fat	1 g
Trans fatty acids, total	0 g
Polyunsaturated fat	2 g
Monounsaturated fat	4.5 g
Cholesterol	30 mg
Sodium	170 mg
Carbohydrate	28 g
Dietary fiber	1 g
Sugars	14 g
Protein	4 g

TIP *Invest in an oven thermometer to make sure your oven is heating properly. Check the temperature in different areas of your oven to make sure it has consistent heat. A hanging mercury thermometer is most reliable. If you notice heating discrepancies, adjust your cooking time or temperature to compensate. Most utility companies can recalibrate your oven, if necessary.*

ON-THE-GO CINNAMON-APPLE TOPPING

For a quick breakfast treat, spread these spiced apples on a whole grain waffle or English muffin topped with peanut butter. They're also delicious mixed into plain yogurt or oatmeal. You can even serve this to your kids as a dessert!

Use a Golden Delicious, Granny Smith, or other baking apple of your choice.

Don't worry if there's a little excess water after microwaving. Most of it will reabsorb as the apple cools.

2 SERVINGS

1 apple, peeled, cored, and cut into 1-inch pieces

2 teaspoons light brown sugar

$1/8$ teaspoon ground cinnamon

1 teaspoon water

In a bowl, combine the apple, brown sugar, cinnamon, and water. Cover with plastic wrap and microwave on high for 2 minutes, stirring after 1 minute. Remove the plastic wrap carefully and stir. Set aside to cool for 5 minutes.

PER SERVING

Calories	50
Calories from fat	0
Fat	0 g
Saturated fat	0 g
Trans fatty acids, total	0 g
Polyunsaturated fat	0 g
Monounsaturated fat	0 g
Cholesterol	0 mg
Sodium	1 mg
Carbohydrate	13 g
Dietary fiber	1 g
Sugars	11 g
Protein	0 g

APPLE-FIG MUESLI

Muesli falls somewhere between granola and oatmeal. Like granola, it is made with oats and dried fruit and served with milk or yogurt. Like oatmeal, the oats are unadulterated, not baked with added fats and sugars. The main difference is that it is prepared ahead of time and served chilled, so it's very refreshing on a warm day.

Though you can purchase premade muesli to "rehydrate" at home, you can also make it yourself easily, mixing oats with spices and fruit, adding liquid, and refrigerating it overnight. Then it's ready for you in the morning to eat or take for later.

If you love Fig Newtons, you'll love dried calimyrna figs. They are so sweet, you'll feel like you're eating a cookie! The same goes for majool dates; these dried fruits are so sweet and creamy they can take the place of dessert.

2 SERVINGS

1/2 cup quick-cooking (not instant) oats

1/2 apple, peeled, cored, and finely chopped

2 fresh or dried figs (preferably calimyrna) or pitted dates (preferably majool), chopped

Pinch salt

1 to 2 pinches ground cinnamon

1 cup low-fat milk, unsweetened almond milk, or soy milk

2 teaspoons honey

Chopped nuts, raisins, sliced bananas, optional

In a bowl, combine the oats, apple, figs, salt, and cinnamon. Add milk and stir to combine. Cover and refrigerate overnight. Before eating, stir, drizzle with honey, and add desired toppings.

PER SERVING	
Calories	210
Calories from fat	25
Fat	2.5 g
Saturated fat	1 g
Trans fatty acids, total	0 g
Polyunsaturated fat	0.5 g
Monounsaturated fat	1 g
Cholesterol	5 mg
Sodium	55 mg
Carbohydrate	40 g
Dietary fiber	4 g
Sugars	25 g
Protein	7 g

If you want, top your muesli with raisins, nuts, or any fresh fruit you have on hand before eating. You can even mix it into Greek yogurt, just as you would granola, for added protein.

BANANA-YOGURT MUFFINS

In these aromatic muffins, canola oil and nonfat yogurt replace the butter and sour cream used in many bakery muffins. Use bananas that are overripe for more concentrated banana flavor.

12 MUFFINS

2/3 cup all-purpose flour

2/3 cup whole wheat flour

1/2 cup granulated sugar

1 teaspoon baking soda

1 teaspoon baking powder

1/2 teaspoon salt

1 egg

3 very ripe bananas

1/2 cup canola oil

1/2 cup nonfat plain Greek or regular yogurt

2 tablespoons chopped walnuts, granola, or mini chocolate chips, optional

Preheat the oven to 350 degrees.

Coat a muffin tin with nonstick cooking spray or fill with liners.

In a bowl, combine both flours, sugar, baking soda, baking powder, and salt.

In a bowl, beat the egg. Add the bananas and mash with a potato masher or fork. Add the oil and yogurt and stir well to combine. Add to the flour mixture and stir gently until just combined. Spoon the batter evenly into the muffin cups. Sprinkle with walnuts, granola, or chocolate chips, if desired.

Bake for 25 to 30 minutes, or until the tops just bounce back when touched. Leave in the tin for 5 to 10 minutes before removing the muffins to a cooling rack.

PER SERVING (one muffin)

Calories	200
Calories from fat	90
Fat	10 g
Saturated fat	1 g
Trans fatty acids, total	0 g
Polyunsaturated fat	2.5 g
Monounsaturated fat	6 g
Cholesterol	15 mg
Sodium	240 mg
Carbohydrate	26 g
Dietary fiber	2 g
Sugars	13 g
Protein	4 g

NOTES

SNACKS

CARROT-APPLE-GINGER JUICE

Making your own juice at home will cost you a fraction of what bottled refrigerated juices cost. For ease of preparation, chop the ingredients in a food processor first and then transfer them to a blender to liquefy.

1 SERVING

4 carrots, finely chopped

1 apple, peeled, cored, and finely chopped

1 (2-inch) piece peeled fresh ginger, finely chopped

1 cup boiling water

1/2 cup 100 percent apple juice

In a blender, combine the carrots, apple, ginger, and boiling water and let sit for 10 minutes. Add the apple juice and blend until liquefied. Refrigerate for an hour or more.

Pour the mixture through a strainer, discarding the solids before drinking.

PER SERVING

Calories	220
Calories from fat	10
Fat	1 g
Saturated fat	0 g
Trans fatty acids, total	0 g
Polyunsaturated fat	0.5 g
Monounsaturated fat	0 g
Cholesterol	0 mg
Sodium	190 mg
Carbohydrate	55 g
Dietary fiber	3 g
Sugars	35 g
Protein	3 g

Experiment with making your own juices using different fruits and vegetables. High-powered Vitamix blenders are designed to juice fruits and vegetables even more quickly.

ROASTED CARROT HUMMUS

Adding roasted carrots to homemade hummus provides a boost of beta carotene, as well as fiber and subtle flavor. Roasting the garlic cuts its sharpness.

Snack on the hummus with sliced veggies and pita or use in the Greek Pita "Taco" (page 112) or Soft-Boiled Eggs on Toast with Hummus and Hot Sauce (page 167).

2 ¼ CUPS

4 carrots, halved lengthwise and cut into ½-inch pieces

1 teaspoon olive oil

3 unpeeled garlic cloves

1 (15-ounce) can chickpeas, rinsed and drained

¼ cup tahini

Juice of 1 lemon

3 tablespoons hot water

3 tablespoons extra-virgin olive oil

1 teaspoon ground cumin, or to taste

1 teaspoon salt, or to taste

Preheat the oven to 400 degrees.

Lightly coat a foil-lined, rimmed baking sheet with nonstick cooking spray.

Place the carrots on the sheet pan, drizzle with the oil, and stir to combine. Evenly distribute the carrots on the baking sheet. Roast for 20 minutes, stirring after 10 minutes. Add the garlic and roast for 10 to 15 minutes, or until the carrots are tender and slightly charred. Set aside to cool briefly and peel the garlic, discarding the skin.

In a food processor, combine the chickpeas, tahini, lemon juice, water, extra-virgin olive oil, cumin, salt, carrots, and garlic until smooth. Adjust seasonings, if desired. If the hummus is too thick, add water, tahini, or lemon juice.

PER SERVING (2 tablespoons)

Calories	70
Calories from fat	40
Fat	4.5 g
Saturated fat	0.5 g
Trans fatty acids, total	0 g
Polyunsaturated fat	1 g
Monounsaturated fat	2.5 g
Cholesterol	0 mg
Sodium	170 mg
Carbohydrate	6 g
Dietary fiber	2 g
Sugars	1 g
Protein	2 g

TIP *Use extra tahini in the Lentil Salad with Tahini Dressing (page 117).*

ROASTED BANANA WITH PB&C

A campfire classic comes inside for a quick and decadent-seeming snack, which actually provides a healthy balance of fruit, protein, and carbohydrates. Use a banana that is ripe and flavorful, but still firm.

If needed, substitute one tablespoon of chocolate chips for the chocolate bar pieces. If you want to avoid chocolate, use raisins. Cooking the banana in its peel provides a built-in "bowl."

1 SERVING

1 ripe, firm unpeeled banana

2 teaspoons peanut butter, preferably all natural

1/2 ounce chocolate (3 squares of a Hershey bar), broken into pieces

Preheat the oven to 400 degrees.

Slice halfway through the banana on the inside curved side. Gently pull the banana partway open and spread with the peanut butter. Insert pieces of chocolate through the length of the banana. Gently push the banana halves back together and wrap in foil. Bake for 8 minutes for a still firm banana or 10 to 15 minutes for a softer banana.

PER SERVING

Calories	260
Calories from fat	90
Fat	10 g
Saturated fat	4 g
Trans fatty acids, total	0 g
Polyunsaturated fat	2 g
Monounsaturated fat	3.5 g
Cholesterol	Less than 5 mg
Sodium	10 mg
Carbohydrate	40 g
Dietary fiber	4 g
Sugars	23 g
Protein	5 g

MOCK BANANA PUDDING

This snack won't fool a true banana pudding aficionado, but for those looking for a healthier take on this classic dessert, try substituting rich and creamy flavored Greek yogurt for the custard, and layer with the traditional banana slices and a few crumbled cookies. Use the classic vanilla wafers, biscotti, ladyfingers, or whole wheat digestives or biscuits for a little extra fiber.

Feel free to squirt a little canned whipped cream on top to entice younger eaters to give it a try.

1 SERVING

1 (5- to 6-ounce) container nonfat banana, vanilla, or honey Greek yogurt

3 vanilla wafers, crumbled, or 2 tablespoons crumbled cookies

$^1/_3$ banana, thinly sliced

Place half of the yogurt in a 6-ounce ramekin or other small bowl. Top with the cookies, the bananas, and the remaining yogurt. Smooth the top and cover with plastic wrap and refrigerate for 3 or more hours.

PER SERVING	
Calories	220
Calories from fat	20
Fat	2.5 g
Saturated fat	0.5 g
Trans fatty acids, total	0 g
Polyunsaturated fat	0.5 g
Monounsaturated fat	1 g
Cholesterol	10 mg
Sodium	105 mg
Carbohydrate	35 g
Dietary fiber	1 g
Sugars	26 g
Protein	14 g

PIZZA-DILLA

When it's just you and you want something filling to eat quickly, it doesn't get any easier than this five-minute tortilla pizza. Cooking it first on the stovetop gets the bottom nice and crispy, and browning it under the broiler gets the top bubbly and gooey in about a minute.

The toppings are limited only by your imagination; try a selection of veggies or other types of cheese.

1 SERVING

1 (8- to 10-inch) whole wheat or flour tortilla

1/4 teaspoon olive oil

2 to 3 tablespoons pizza or marinara sauce

1/2 cup shredded mozzarella cheese

1 tablespoon freshly grated Parmesan cheese

Preheat the broiler to high and set an oven rack 6 to 8 inches from the heat.

Preheat a cast iron or heavy ovenproof skillet on the stove over high heat. Brush one side of the tortilla with the oil. Place the tortilla oil-side down in the skillet and spread with pizza sauce. Cover with the mozzarella, sprinkle with Parmesan, and cook for 30 seconds. Place the skillet under the broiler for 1 minute, or until cheese is melted and starting to brown and bubble, checking frequently after 30 seconds. Carefully remove the skillet from the oven. Transfer the tortilla to a cutting board and set aside to cool briefly before cutting.

PER SERVING

Calories	350
Calories from fat	150
Fat	17 g
Saturated fat	9 g
Trans fatty acids, total	0 g
Polyunsaturated fat	1 g
Monounsaturated fat	5 g
Cholesterol	40 mg
Sodium	810 mg
Carbohydrate	28 g
Dietary fiber	6 g
Sugars	3 g
Protein	21 g

TIP *Note that the oven rack is not at the highest position for this recipe. After removing the hot pan from the oven, immediately put an oven mitt over its handle so that you don't accidently grab it and burn yourself.*

ICY CHOCOLATE SHAKE

When you're craving a chocolate milk shake, try this lighter version made with chocolate syrup, low-fat milk, and ice cubes. It whips up to deliver a frosty chocolate drink in seconds and is especially refreshing after exercising or in hot weather.

1 SERVING

1 cup ice cubes

1 cup low-fat milk

2 tablespoons chocolate syrup

In a blender, combine the ice cubes, milk, and chocolate syrup and blend until frothy.

PER SERVING

Calories	210
Calories from fat	25
Fat	3 g
Saturated fat	1.5 g
Trans fatty acids, total	0 g
Polyunsaturated fat	0 g
Monounsaturated fat	1 g
Cholesterol	10 mg
Sodium	140 mg
Carbohydrate	38 g
Dietary fiber	1 g
Sugars	32 g
Protein	9 g

If you need a protein boost, add a tablespoon of peanut butter. For a mocha treat, add a couple of ice cubes made from leftover coffee. For a coffee shake, use ice cubes made from coffee and substitute sugar for the chocolate syrup.

MIXED BERRY SMOOTHIE

A convenient way to incorporate fruit and protein-filled dairy into your daily diet is to combine them in a refreshing drink, which is great as a snack, for breakfast, or as a lunch on the run.

Even kids who turn up their noses at fresh fruit or plain yogurt will change their tune when presented with a frosty shake. They don't have to know it's good for them!

1 SERVING

1 cup frozen mixed berries

1 (5- to 6-ounce) container nonfat plain or vanilla Greek yogurt

1/2 cup 100 percent apple or orange juice

In a blender, combine the berries, yogurt, and juice and blend until smooth.

PER SERVING

Calories	210
Calories from fat	0
Fat	0.5 g
Saturated fat	0 g
Trans fatty acids, total	0 g
Polyunsaturated fat	0 g
Monounsaturated fat	0 g
Cholesterol	0 mg
Sodium	65 mg
Carbohydrate	36 g
Dietary fiber	6 g
Sugars	27 g
Protein	16 g

TIP *Keep bags of frozen fruit on hand and freeze any fresh berries or fruit that are going to go bad before they're eaten. Experiment with combinations of berries and fruit. If you find yourself with fresh fruit to use up, throw in a couple of ice cubes to frost it up.*

NO-COOK GRANOLA BARS

These five-ingredient bars are convenient to have on hand for a quick snack. They can be delicate, so keep them in the refrigerator and make sure to press them into the pan well. If you do get some crumbles, eat them on their own or add to frozen yogurt for a tasty treat.

Lining the pan with foil makes the mixture easier to remove from the pan before slicing. You can then return them in the foil to the pan to store.

12 BARS

1/2 cup peanut butter

1/3 cup honey

1 cup old-fashioned rolled oats

1 cup trail mix or assorted nuts, seeds and dried fruit

1/4 cup shredded unsweetened or sweetened coconut

In a bowl, combine the peanut butter and honey. Add the oats, trail mix, and coconut and stir to combine.

Transfer the mixture to an 8-by-8-inch baking dish lined with aluminum foil. With moistened hands, press down well on the mixture to compact it. Refrigerate for 3 or more hours. Cut into bars and serve immediately or keep refrigerated.

PER SERVING (one bar)

Calories	180
Calories from fat	100
Fat	11 g
Saturated fat	2.5 g
Trans fatty acids, total	0 g
Polyunsaturated fat	3 g
Monounsaturated fat	4.5 g
Cholesterol	0 mg
Sodium	80 mg
Carbohydrate	18 g
Dietary fiber	2 g
Sugars	9 g
Protein	5 g

You can adapt these bars by using a different kind of nut butter or varying the mix-ins: any combination of nuts, dried fruits, and seeds works well. To make it super easy, use a prepared or packaged nut and dried fruit mix that includes a variety of nuts, seeds, and raisins. (Just make sure it's fresh and fragrant. If kept too long in a package, the mixture can absorb odors and will eventually turn rancid.) For kids (or adults with a bit of a sweet tooth), add a sprinkling of chocolate chips.

KALE CHIPS

This crunchy snack is just as addictive as potato chips but a lot healthier, because it is made with less oil and baked, not fried.

It's important to massage the oil into the leaves to tenderize them, so prepare to get your hands messy. To prevent soggy chips, dry the kale completely after washing (if you're not using the prewashed variety). Remove the tough stems, which can be bitter.

If you prefer milder flavor, skip the onion powder and garlic powder. Keep in mind the leaves will shrink dramatically during baking, so flavors will intensify.

6 SERVINGS

1 pound kale, preferably Tuscan or lacinato, thick ribs removed, cut into 1-inch pieces

1 tablespoon olive oil

Onion powder

Garlic powder

Kosher or sea salt

Preheat the oven to 275 degrees.

Lightly coat two foil-lined, rimmed baking sheets with nonstick cooking spray.

In a bowl, combine the kale and oil. Using your hands, massage the kale, rubbing the leaves to soften and coat with the oil. Sprinkle lightly with onion powder, garlic powder, and salt. Massage again to coat.

Place the kale pieces on the baking sheet. Bake for 30 minutes, or until crisp, flipping the chips after 15 minutes.

PER SERVING

Calories	40
Calories from fat	25
Fat	2.5 g
Saturated fat	0.5 g
Trans fatty acids, total	0 g
Polyunsaturated fat	0.5 g
Monounsaturated fat	1.5 g
Cholesterol	0 mg
Sodium	20 mg
Carbohydrate	4 g
Dietary fiber	2 g
Sugars	1 g
Protein	2 g

TIP *When possible choose lacinato kale, also known as dinosaur or Tuscan kale, instead of curly kale. It's more tender and flavorful and has less grit.*

ON-THE-GO SNACK MIX

When making your own snack mix, balance is key, both from a nutritional and taste/texture perspective. In this recipe, the combination of protein-packed, calorie-dense nuts and dried fruits with lower-calorie complex carbohydrates achieves the right balance of salty, sweet, chewy, and crunchy. Popcorn is high in fiber and serves as the base of this mix. However, even popcorn has calories and should not be consumed with abandon!

Instead of pretzels, you can substitute another type of small cracker or even a high-fiber cereal, such as Unfrosted Mini Wheats, Crackling Bran, or Wheat Chex.

Make a batch each week to have on hand to prevent hunger and eventual overeating when you are running around and delay or skip a meal.

7 SERVINGS

4 cups air-popped popcorn

1 cup small pretzels, crackers, or high-fiber cereal

$^1/_2$ cup almonds

$^1/_2$ cup peanuts

$^1/_2$ cup raisins

$^1/_2$ cup dried sweetened cranberries

In a container with an airtight lid, combine the popcorn, pretzels, almonds, peanuts, raisins, and cranberries.

PER SERVING

Calories	220
Calories from fat	100
Fat	11 g
Saturated fat	1 g
Trans fatty acids, total	0 g
Polyunsaturated fat	3 g
Monounsaturated fat	6 g
Cholesterol	0 mg
Sodium	160 mg
Carbohydrate	28 g
Dietary fiber	4 g
Sugars	13 g
Protein	6 g

TIP *Homemade snack mixes are so convenient for taking to kids' sports events and to have on hand when you need something to eat in a hurry. They are also a great way to use up almost empty boxes or bags of cereal, small crackers, nuts, or dried fruit. Choose a combination of unsalted and salted and roasted and raw nuts for balance.*

DESSERTS

HONEY-RASPBERRY FROZEN YOGURT

When you feel like a blast of summer flavor in the middle of winter, try this homemade frozen yogurt. It has such vibrant berry flavor, you'll be licking your bowl. It's delicious enough to serve for company, and they'll never believe you made it yourself!

Frozen fruit package sizes keep getting smaller, so the berries you find may be in twelve-ounce packages instead of sixteen-ounce packages. Either will work.

If there are any leftovers, transfer the frozen yogurt into a freezer-safe container with a lid.

4 SERVINGS

1 (12- or 16-ounce) package frozen raspberries

1 cup nonfat plain or vanilla Greek yogurt

2 tablespoons honey

In a microwave on 30 percent power, defrost the raspberries for 1 minute. They will still feel frozen.

In a food processor, combine the raspberries, yogurt, and honey and process until creamy and smooth, scraping down the sides if necessary. Serve immediately.

PER SERVING	
Calories	100
Calories from fat	0
Fat	0 g
Saturated fat	0 g
Trans fatty acids, total	0 g
Polyunsaturated fat	0 g
Monounsaturated fat	0 g
Cholesterol	0 mg
Sodium	25 mg
Carbohydrate	18 g
Dietary fiber	Less than 1 g
Sugars	18 g
Protein	6 g

A serving of some brands of Greek yogurt provides a quarter of your daily calcium requirement and more than 40 percent of your daily recommendation of protein.

CHOCOLATE FRUIT AND NUT BARK

When you make your own chocolate bar, you can customize it however you'd like. This combination features salted almonds, tart dried cherries and cranberries, crystallized ginger, and raisins for complex taste variations. You can substitute other nuts and fruits; try for about three-quarters to one cup of add-ins.

As any chocoholic will confirm, dark chocolate has health properties: it contains good-for-you antioxidants. Sadly, it also is high in calories and should be consumed in moderation.

After chopping the nuts, put them in a strainer and discard excess nut particles and dust.

8 TO 10 SERVINGS

7 ounces bittersweet chocolate, chopped

1/3 cup chopped roasted salted almonds

2 tablespoons finely chopped crystallized ginger

1 heaping tablespoon dried cherries

1 heaping tablespoon dried sweetened cranberries

1 heaping tablespoon raisins

Place the chocolate in a microwave-safe bowl. Microwave on high for 2 to 3 minutes, stirring at 1 minute and then at 15-second intervals, until smooth (when it is almost melted, stir until smooth instead of heating again). Add the almonds, ginger, cherries, cranberries, and raisins, stirring until combined.

Lightly coat a foil-lined baking sheet with nonstick cooking spray. Mark a 7-by-10-inch section and spread the chocolate evenly over that area. Refrigerate for 1 or more hours. Break into pieces and serve immediately or keep refrigerated.

PER SERVING

Calories	170
Calories from fat	120
Fat	13 g
Saturated fat	6 g
Trans fatty acids, total	0 g
Polyunsaturated fat	1 g
Monounsaturated fat	6 g
Cholesterol	0 mg
Sodium	20 mg
Carbohydrate	19 g
Dietary fiber	2 g
Sugars	14 g
Protein	3 g

 Use a high-quality chocolate bar you like eating on its own. Some bars come in increments of 3 ounces; others come in 3.5-ounce sizes. If you are using 6 ounces, just add slightly less fruit.

FROZEN BANANAS THREE WAYS

I often find myself with one or two extra bananas—not enough to make muffins but enough to make these shockingly easy desserts. Make sure your bananas are ripe, firm, and flavorful enough to eat as is, not underripe or overripe and mushy.

CHOCOLATE-COVERED FROZEN BANANAS

Keeping these small treats in your freezer can help you make a better choice when that pint of ice cream is calling your name. Another plus: because they are frozen, it takes longer to eat your way through them, giving you time to get cravings back on track. For added flavor, roll the bananas in chopped nuts or toasted coconut after coating them with chocolate.

3 SERVINGS

1 ounce chopped bittersweet chocolate or 1/4 cup chocolate chips

1/4 teaspoon canola oil

2 ripe, firm bananas, cut into thirds

1 tablespoon chopped peanuts or toasted shredded coconut, optional

Combine the chocolate and oil in a microwave-safe bowl. Microwave on high, stirring at 45 seconds and then at 10-second increments until smooth (when it is almost melted, stir until smooth instead of heating again). Holding a banana piece with a fork or skewer, roll in chocolate to coat. Sprinkle with nuts or coconut, if desired. Place the pieces on a wax- or parchment paper–covered plate. Repeat with remaining pieces and freeze for 4 hours or more.

PER SERVING	
Calories	130
Calories from fat	40
Fat	4.5 g
Saturated fat	2 g
Trans fatty acids, total	0 g
Polyunsaturated fat	0.5 g
Monounsaturated fat	2 g
Cholesterol	0 mg
Sodium	0 mg
Carbohydrate	24 g
Dietary fiber	3 g
Sugars	14 g
Protein	2 g

BANANA "ICE CREAM"

Few would believe that a plain frozen banana puréed in a food processor could make a creamy ice cream–like dessert. This is one you have to try!

2 SERVINGS

3 ripe, firm bananas, sliced

Place the banana slices on a wax paper– or parchment paper–covered plate and freeze for 4 or more hours. Place the bananas in a food processor and process until creamy and smooth, scraping down the sides if necessary.

PER SERVING

Calories	170
Calories from fat	5
Fat	0.5 g
Saturated fat	0 g
Trans fatty acids, total	0 g
Polyunsaturated fat	0 g
Monounsaturated fat	0 g
Cholesterol	0 mg
Sodium	0 mg
Carbohydrate	43 g
Dietary fiber	5 g
Sugars	23 g
Protein	2 g

BANANA-CHOCOLATE "ICE CREAM"

In this variation, chocolate-covered banana slices are puréed to make an icy treat that tastes decadent but isn't.

2 SERVINGS

1 ounce ($^{1}/_{4}$ cup) chopped bittersweet chocolate or semisweet chips

$^{1}/_{4}$ teaspoon canola oil

2 ripe, firm bananas, cut into thirds

Combine the chocolate and oil in a microwave-safe bowl. Microwave on high, stirring at 45 seconds and then at 10-second increments until smooth (when it is almost melted, stir until smooth instead of heating again). Holding a banana piece with a fork or skewer, roll in chocolate to coat. Place on a wax- or parchment paper–covered plate. Repeat with remaining pieces and freeze for 4 or more hours. Place the banana and any extra frozen chocolate in a food processor and process until creamy and smooth, scraping down the sides if necessary.

PER SERVING

Calories	190
Calories from fat	60
Fat	7 g
Saturated fat	3 g
Trans fatty acids, total	0 g
Polyunsaturated fat	0.5 g
Monounsaturated fat	3 g
Cholesterol	0 mg
Sodium	0 mg
Carbohydrate	36 g
Dietary fiber	4 g
Sugars	21 g
Protein	2 g

CHOCOLATE CHIP MERINGUES

These bite-sized cookies will satisfy "cookie monsters" of all ages by providing crunch and sweetness in one bite—maybe two if you're delicate! Don't be intimidated if you've never attempted a meringue before; just keep beating until the egg whites become thick and glossy.

If you like a slightly chewier meringue, take the cookies out of the oven just after baking instead of letting them sit for the additional half hour.

60 COOKIES

3 egg whites
$1/4$ teaspoon cream of tartar

$3/4$ cup granulated sugar
1 teaspoon vanilla extract

$1/2$ cup mini or regular chocolate chips or finely chopped bittersweet chocolate

Preheat the oven to 300 degrees.

Line two baking sheets with parchment paper, securing the edges with tape.

With an electric mixer, beat the egg whites and cream of tartar until soft peaks form. Gradually add the sugar, 1 tablespoon at a time, until thick and glossy. Add the vanilla. Gently fold in chips.

Place the mixture in a pastry bag fitted with a $1/2$- or $3/4$-inch tip. Pipe 1-inch rounds onto the parchment, leaving 1 to 2 inches between cookies. With damp fingertips, press down any peaks.

Bake for 25 to 30 minutes, or until lightly golden and firm, rotating pans halfway through baking. Turn off heat and leave in the oven for 30 minutes.

PER SERVING (one cookie)	
Calories	20
Calories from fat	0
Fat	0.5 g
Saturated fat	0.5 g
Trans fatty acids, total	0 g
Polyunsaturated fat	0 g
Monounsaturated fat	0 g
Cholesterol	0 mg
Sodium	3 mg
Carbohydrate	3 g
Dietary fiber	0 g
Sugars	3 g
Protein	0 g

 Piping the cookies from a pastry bag makes distributing the cookie "batter" easier and faster. If you don't have a pastry bag, use a zip-top bag with a 1/2-inch hole snipped in the bottom corner of the bag. You can also use a tablespoon to drop the batter onto the parchment paper.

DARK CHOCOLATE SORBET

It's hard to believe this rich and creamy chocolate sorbet is dairy-free and a cinch to make. With so few ingredients, it's worth investing in Dutch processed cocoa, which has gone through a process to neutralize its acidity, giving it a darker and smoother finish. Regular cocoa will also be delicious though.

Make sure to use a large saucepan because the mixture bubbles up during cooking. You might also need to adjust the flame to prevent it from overflowing.

Take the sorbet out of the freezer about ten to fifteen minutes before you plan to serve it for easier scooping.

6 SERVINGS

2 1/4 cups water, divided use

1 cup granulated sugar

1/2 cup unsweetened cocoa, preferably Dutch processed

Pinch salt

1 teaspoon vanilla extract

In a large saucepan, bring 1 1/2 cups of the water, sugar, cocoa powder, and salt to a boil for 30 to 45 seconds, whisking constantly to prevent it from overflowing, reducing the heat if necessary. Remove from the heat and add the vanilla and the remaining 3/4 cup of water, whisking to combine. Transfer to a bowl and refrigerate until completely chilled.

Transfer the mixture to an ice cream maker and process according to manufacturer's instructions. (Don't worry if it is still soft, it will continue to harden as it freezes.) Transfer the sorbet into a freezer-safe container with a lid. Freeze for 1 or more hours, or until firm. Remove from the freezer 10 to 15 minutes before serving.

PER SERVING

Calories	150
Calories from fat	10
Fat	1 g
Saturated fat	0.5 g
Trans fatty acids, total	0 g
Polyunsaturated fat	0 g
Monounsaturated fat	0.5 g
Cholesterol	0 mg
Sodium	5 mg
Carbohydrate	38 g
Dietary fiber	2 g
Sugars	34 g
Protein	1 g

Feel free to customize the flavor by adding espresso powder during cooking or a shot of espresso or coffee liquor before freezing.

POMEGRANATE-GINGER GRANITA

For those who are unfamiliar with a granita, it's a refreshing icy concoction made with sugar, water, and flavorings. Its light and airy texture makes it the perfect after-dinner treat when you want something sweet but not heavy or overly filling. Here, pomegranate juice is infused with a flavored simple syrup to add a hint of ginger.

To achieve the granita's signature slushy consistency, stir it frequently during the freezing process to keep the mixture from becoming a solid block. You can refreeze any leftover granita in a freezer-safe container with a lid.

6 SERVINGS

½ cup boiling water

1 (3-inch) piece peeled fresh ginger, chopped

½ cup granulated sugar

3 cups 100 percent pomegranate juice

In a measuring cup, combine the water and ginger. Steep for 30 minutes. Strain into a larger bowl, discarding the ginger. Add the sugar and stir until dissolved (if it doesn't dissolve easily, heat the mixture slightly and stir to dissolve). In a bowl, combine the simple syrup and the pomegranate juice and stir to combine.

Pour into a 13-by-9-inch baking pan. Freeze for 1 to 2 hours, or until the edges and bottom turn to ice. Using a fork, scrape the sides and bottom and stir to redistribute. Return to the freezer and repeat every 30 to 60 minutes for 2 to 4 hours, or until the mixture is icy and light. Continue to scrape the mixture occasionally until serving.

PER SERVING

Calories	130
Calories from fat	0
Fat	0.5 g
Saturated fat	0 g
Trans fatty acids, total	0 g
Polyunsaturated fat	0 g
Monounsaturated fat	0 g
Cholesterol	0 mg
Sodium	10 mg
Carbohydrate	33 g
Dietary fiber	0 g
Sugars	32 g
Protein	0 g

Feel free to adapt this recipe by using any strongly flavored juice (grapefruit is another favorite). You can even make it with coffee. If you have leftover pomegranate juice, use it in a smoothie.

LEMON-ROSEMARY SORBET

Sorbets are an elegant way to end a meal and require very little work. They are satisfyingly sweet but not overindulgent. Fresh rosemary adds an herbal note to this refreshing lemony after-dinner treat.

4 SERVINGS

1 ½ cups water

1 cup plus 2 tablespoons granulated sugar

Zest of 1 lemon

2 (4-inch) sprigs fresh rosemary

¾ cup fresh lemon juice

In a saucepan, combine the water, sugar, lemon zest, and rosemary. Bring to a boil, swirling the pot to combine. Reduce the heat and simmer for 5 minutes. Set aside to cool completely, 1 or more hours. Strain into a larger bowl, discarding the rosemary. Add the lemon juice and stir to combine. Refrigerate until completely chilled.

Transfer the mixture into an ice cream maker and process according to manufacturer's instructions. Serve immediately or transfer the sorbet into a freezer-safe container with a lid.

PER SERVING

Calories	230
Calories from fat	0
Fat	0 g
Saturated fat	0 g
Trans fatty acids, total	0 g
Polyunsaturated fat	0 g
Monounsaturated fat	0 g
Cholesterol	0 mg
Sodium	15 mg
Carbohydrate	59 g
Dietary fiber	0 g
Sugars	57 g
Protein	0 g

MELON AND BERRIES WITH MINT

Especially in the warmer months, a bowl or platter of fresh fruit is a welcome dessert, but sometimes it just needs a little boost. Fresh mint and a squeeze of lime give this dessert the zing you are looking for.

5 SERVINGS

2 tablespoons fresh lime juice

1 tablespoon honey

1 tablespoon chopped fresh mint

2 cups cubed cantaloupe

2 cups cubed honeydew

1 cup fresh raspberries

In a large bowl, combine the lime juice, honey, and mint. Add the cantaloupe, honeydew, and raspberries and stir gently to coat well.

PER SERVING	
Calories	70
Calories from fat	0
Fat	0.5 g
Saturated fat	0 g
Trans fatty acids, total	0 g
Polyunsaturated fat	0 g
Monounsaturated fat	0 g
Cholesterol	0 mg
Sodium	24 mg
Carbohydrate	18 g
Dietary fiber	3 g
Sugars	15 g
Protein	1 g

 Make sure the fruit is ripe and flavorful. If raspberries aren't available, use strawberries.

ROASTED PINEAPPLE WITH TOASTED COCONUT

Roasting fruit intensifies its natural sweetness. Luckily for most of us, sweet fresh pineapple is available almost year-round, and a sprinkle of cinnamon-sugar easily takes it from a snack to dessert.

Here, the pineapple is paired with creamy Greek yogurt mixed with a little honey, but you can also serve it with flavored yogurt, frozen vanilla yogurt, or sorbet.

Toast the coconut in the oven or toaster oven at 350 degrees, stirring frequently and watching carefully to prevent burning.

4 SERVINGS

- 1 peeled and cored pineapple, cut into eight (^{1}/2-inch) rounds
- 2 tablespoons light brown sugar
- ^{1}/2 teaspoon ground cinnamon
- Pinch salt
- 2 cups nonfat plain Greek yogurt
- 2 tablespoons honey
- 2 tablespoons shredded unsweetened or sweetened coconut, toasted

Preheat the oven to 450 degrees.

Line a rimmed baking sheet with parchment paper and place the pineapple slices on top.

In a bowl, combine the brown sugar, cinnamon, and salt. Sprinkle on top of the pineapple. Roast for 15 to 20 minutes, or until golden brown around the edges.

Meanwhile, in a bowl, combine the yogurt and honey and stir until smooth. In individual bowls, place two slices of pineapple, top with a dollop of yogurt, and sprinkle with coconut.

PER SERVING

Calories	200
Calories from fat	15
Fat	2 g
Saturated fat	1.5 g
Trans fatty acids, total	0 g
Polyunsaturated fat	0 g
Monounsaturated fat	0 g
Cholesterol	0 mg
Sodium	50 mg
Carbohydrate	35 g
Dietary fiber	2 g
Sugars	31 g
Protein	12 g

TIP *Nonfat Greek yogurt provides twice the protein and has almost 50 percent less sugar, carbs, and sodium than regular nonfat yogurt.*

EXTRAS

ROASTED CHICKEN BREASTS

Turn to this recipe when you want to have chicken breasts ready to use in salads, sandwiches, soups, and stews, including the Four-Pepper Chicken Chili (page 59), Chicken-Black Bean "Tamale" Casserole (page 43), or Barbecue Chicken Sandwiches (page 103). Or, you can cook and eat as is for a healthy main course and serve with an interesting side dish!

Always let poultry and meat rest for five to ten minutes after cooking. If you'll be using it in a cold or room temperature dish, allow it to cool before shredding the meat. Discard the bones and skin.

2 to 4 bone-in, skin-on chicken breasts

Salt and freshly ground black pepper

Preheat the oven to 350 degrees.

Lightly coat a foil-lined, rimmed baking sheet with nonstick cooking spray. Place the chicken breasts on the baking sheet, skin side up. Sprinkle with salt and pepper. Roast for 45 to 50 minutes, or until cooked through. Let rest for 5 to 10 minutes before slicing.

PER SERVING

(one chicken breast)

Calories	370
Calories from fat	70
Fat	8 g
Saturated fat	2.5 g
Trans fatty acids, total	0.0 g
Polyunsaturated fat	1.5 g
Monounsaturated fat	3.0 g
Cholesterol	190 mg
Sodium	170 mg
Carbohydrate	0 g
Dietary fiber	0 g
Sugars	0 g
Protein	69 g

 TIP *While this recipe is for chicken breasts, you can follow it for roasting other parts of the chicken, as well. Even when cooking with all white meat (or all dark meat), it's important to adjust the cooking time if you have pieces of greatly varying sizes. Larger pieces will take longer to cook than smaller ones (sometimes an exceptionally big breast will take 50 percent more time than a small piece). Not sure when chicken is done? An instant-read thermometer inserted into the thickest part of the meat should register 165 degrees, the meat should feel firm to the touch, and the juices should run clear, not pink.*

BALSAMIC VINAIGRETTE

Store-bought salad dressings are notorious for hiding sugar and salt. Using, and especially overusing, heavy, fat-laden dressings overwhelms the beautiful combination of greens and vegetables in salads and adds unnecessary calories.

Making your own vinaigrette takes less than five minutes. Make a batch every week and use it judiciously. You just want to coat the greens to add vibrancy and bring out their flavor, not overwhelm them.

Treat yourself to good quality extra-virgin olive oil for salad dressings. Try different brands to find the one you like the most. Save money by using regular olive oil or canola oil for cooking and splurge when flavor really matters.

Also experiment with using different vinegars, including red wine, white balsamic, and sherry vinegars, which all provide subtle differences in flavor. Discover your favorite combinations and you will never go back to the salad dressing aisle in the supermarket.

MAKES 1 CUP

1/2 cup balsamic vinegar

1 tablespoon Dijon mustard

1 teaspoon granulated sugar

1/2 cup extra-virgin olive oil

Salt and freshly ground black pepper

In a bowl, combine the vinegar, mustard, and sugar. Slowly whisk in the oil to incorporate (or put into a jar and shake well). Season with salt and pepper.

PER SERVING (1 tablespoon)

Calories	70
Calories from fat	60
Fat	7 g
Saturated fat	1 g
Trans fatty acids, total	0 g
Polyunsaturated fat	0.5 g
Monounsaturated fat	5 g
Cholesterol	0 mg
Sodium	25 mg
Carbohydrate	2 g
Dietary fiber	0 g
Sugars	1 g
Protein	0 g

TIP *We've all heard the expression "like oil and water." That applies to salad dressing, too. If not combined correctly, the oil and vinegar will separate; that's why slowly whisking the olive oil into a binder, such as mustard, helps it emulsify. A great tool for making lush salad dressings is a milk frother, which looks like a little electric whisk. It's often sold for making cappuccinos at home, but it also works well to quickly bind vinaigrettes.*

CHICKEN BROTH TWO WAYS

Substituting broth for water adds flavor to any dish, from rice to soup to gravy. Try making your own broth; it's preservative free, much lower in sodium than the store-bought variety, and more economical. But who can be blamed for not wanting to be tethered to the kitchen while the bones slowly simmer on the stove for hours? Now you don't have to be. You can get the same results by using a slow cooker. Just put the few ingredients together in the morning and it's ready to go by dinner. Even better, make it a day ahead of time and refrigerate the broth, so the fat has time to rise to the top and harden for easy removal.

You can use chicken wings for this recipe, or many stores sell meaty backs and other bones for a fraction of the cost of a whole chicken. If you don't see them displayed, ask the butcher to put some aside for you.

Because every slow cooker's temperature varies a bit, trust your nose to tell you when the broth is ready; the aroma will go from "hmmm, something's cooking" to a rich and intoxicating poultry scent. It's worth waiting a little longer for more concentrated flavor.

For a richer broth to use in a chicken-based soup or gravy, roast the bones first. Use the lighter version for general cooking.

LIGHT CHICKEN BROTH

Just combine and step away! It doesn't get any easier than that. Keep unused stock in the refrigerator for up to five days or freeze to use later.

MAKES 3 QUARTS

3 pounds meaty chicken bones and/or wings

1 onion, quartered

1 garlic clove, smashed

1 tablespoon salt, preferably kosher

5 black peppercorns

3 quarts water, or more if needed

In a slow-cooker, place the bones, onion, garlic, salt, peppercorns, and water. If the bones are not completely submerged, add more water to cover. Cook on low for 8 to 10 hours or high for 4 to 6, or until you can smell a rich cooked poultry aroma. Set aside to cool. Place a large strainer in a large bowl and carefully transfer the contents of the pot to the strainer, pushing down with a spoon to extract all the liquid. Discard the solids.

PER SERVING (1 cup)

Calories	10
Calories from fat	0
Fat	0.5 g
Saturated fat	0 g
Trans fatty acids, total	0 g
Polyunsaturated fat	0 g
Monounsaturated fat	0 g
Cholesterol	Less than 5 mg
Sodium	360 mg
Carbohydrate	0 g
Dietary fiber	0 g
Sugars	0 g
Protein	1 g

RICH ROASTED BROTH

Most of the fat will melt off the bones as they roast and coat the bottom of the pan, making it easy to remove. Keep unused stock in the refrigerator for up to five days or freeze to use later.

MAKES 3 QUARTS

3 pounds meaty chicken bones and/or wings

2 teaspoons canola oil

1 onion, quartered

1 garlic clove, smashed

1 tablespoon salt, preferably kosher

5 black peppercorns

3 quarts water

Preheat the oven to 375 degrees.

Place the bones in a roasting pan and drizzle with the oil. Bake for 1 to 1 ½ hours, or until the bones are golden brown.

Transfer the bones to a slow cooker, discarding the excess fat. Add the onion, garlic, salt, and peppercorns. Add the water to cover. Cook on low for 8 to 10 hours or high for 4 to 6, or until you can smell a rich poultry aroma. Set aside to cool. Place a large strainer in a large bowl and carefully transfer the contents of the pot to the strainer, pushing down with a spoon to extract all the liquid. Discard the solids.

PER SERVING (1 cup)

Calories	10
Calories from fat	0
Fat	0.5 g
Saturated fat	0 g
Trans fatty acids, total	0 g
Polyunsaturated fat	0 g
Monounsaturated fat	0 g
Cholesterol	Less than 5 mg
Sodium	360 mg
Carbohydrate	0 g
Dietary fiber	0 g
Sugars	0 g
Protein	1 g

DECIPHERING FOOD CLAIMS

Part of evaluating food choices is knowing how to decipher the terms food companies paste on their packaging. Some terms are regulated—meaning if a term is used on a label, it has to mean something specific. But that's not the case for all terms, and it pays to know what's what.

All natural/natural—Not defined or regulated by the FDA, the terms natural and all natural don't really mean very much. Foods labeled natural or all natural won't have added colors, artificial flavors, or synthetic substances, but that doesn't mean that the food is unprocessed or even healthy.

Calorie terms—

- *Low-calorie*—Low-calorie means 40 calories or less per serving.

- *Reduced-calorie*—Reduced-calorie means at least 25 percent fewer calories than the regular version. Check the serving size, though! Reduced-calorie does not mean that you can eat a lot of the food without taking in too many calories.

Fat claims—

- *Fat-free*—Fat-free or 100 percent fat-free means the food contains less than ½ gram of fat per serving.

- *Low-fat*—Low-fat means the food has 3 grams or less per serving.

- *Reduced-fat*—Reduced-fat means the product has 25 percent less fat than the regular version. However, remember that the term reduced-fat is still proportionate to the total fat in the regular version, so it could still contain a lot of fat. Read the label!

Fiber claims—A claim can be made that a food is a "good source" of fiber if it provides 10 percent (2.5 grams) of the Daily Value (25 grams) of fiber per serving. Foods can be called "high in fiber," "rich in fiber," or an "excellent source of fiber" if they contain 20 percent (5 grams) of the daily value of fiber per serving.

Gluten-free—Gluten is a protein found in grains like wheat, rye, and barley, and for people with celiac disease or gluten intolerance, a gluten-free diet can be critical. For other people, however, there is no scientific evidence at this point that a gluten-free diet is healthier.

Light or lite—These terms can be used to refer to fat, calories, or sodium, and the label can mean different things. Generally speaking, if the claim is referring to fat or calories, the product will have either half (or less) of the fat or at least 30 percent fewer calories.

Multigrain—Technically, multigrain means just what you would guess: it contains multiple grains. But those grains can be as refined or processed as the grains in white bread, so it doesn't mean it's necessarily better for you, and it doesn't mean the food is whole grain.

Organic—The term organic refers to plant foods grown without pesticides or genetic modifications. It also refers to meat, poultry, eggs, and dairy products produced without the use of antibiotics or growth hormones.

The USDA makes no claims that organic food is safer or more nutritious than conventionally produced food. Several studies have looked at the nutrient content of organic versus conventionally grown fruits or vegetables, and while some studies suggest a higher nutrient content, others suggest no difference.

The way in which the term organic is used also makes a difference:

- Foods labeled as *100 percent organic* must contain only organically produced ingredients and processing aids, excluding water and salt.

- Foods labeled as *organic* must contain at least 95 percent organically produced ingredients, excluding water and salt.

- A food labeled as *made with organic ingredients* must contain at least 70 percent organic ingredients, excluding water and salt.

Sodium terms—

- *Sodium-free*—A food labeled as sodium-free contains less than 5 mg of sodium per serving. After that, there are many different regulated terms related to sodium, such as *very low sodium* and *low-sodium.*

- *Reduced sodium*—Reduced sodium or less sodium means that the product contains at least 25 percent less sodium than the regular product. *Light in sodium* means the product contains 50 percent less than the standard version. Remember, however, that neither of these mean the food is low in sodium!

Sugar terms—

- *Sugar-free*—A food labeled as sugar-free contains less than ½ g of sugar per serving.

- *Reduced sugar*—Reduced sugar means a product has at least 25 percent less sugar than the regular version, so it could still contain a lot of sugar. These foods may still contain artificial sweeteners.

Two percent milk—Two percent milk sounds good, right? However, most people don't realize that whole milk contains just 3.25 percent fat. Only 1 percent milk and skim milk are considered low-fat. (Skim milk may also be called nonfat or fat-free milk.)

Whole grain—Foods that contain 51 percent or more whole grain ingredients by weight can be labeled as "100 percent whole grain" or may carry the claim that "diets rich in whole grain foods and other plant foods low in total fat, saturated fat, and cholesterol may reduce the risk of heart disease and certain cancers." Don't go by color: dark breads can be made with refined flour and darkening agents like molasses.

Zero trans fat—The FDA requires food manufacturers to list trans fats on the nutritional label, and you may see products in the grocery store boasting that they are free of trans fats. But take heed: legally, the amount on the label can be rounded down to zero if the amount per serving is less than .5 grams. If partially hydrogenated oil is in the ingredient list, the product contains trans fats.

RECIPES BY CATEGORY

READY IN UNDER 30 MINUTES

FAMILY FAVORITES

PREP EARLY, EAT LATER—
MARINATE BEFORE WORK

Chicken Fajitas with Tricolored Peppers (page 84)

Honey-Lime Pork Tenderloin (page 58)

Marinated Flank Steak with Thai Slaw (page 83)

Peanut Chicken Skewers (page 46)

Yogurt- and Spice-Infused Chicken Breasts (page 54)

FARMERS' MARKET FINDS—
WHERE VEGGIES RULE

Arugula and Kale Salad (page 99)

Carrot and Parsnip Soup Two Ways (page 108)

Cauliflower and Leek Soup (page 128)

Chicken Fajitas with Tricolored Peppers (page 84)

Chicken Paillard with Arugula and Fennel (page 66)

Chicken Waldorf Salad (page 125)

Chunky Pasta and Bean Soup (page 114)

Curried Vegetables (page 82)

Easy One-Pot Chicken and Vegetables (page 91)

Eggplant Parmesan Light (page 73)

Farro Salad with Feta and Fresh Herbs (page 98)

Four-Pepper Chicken Chili (page 59)

Fusilli with Broccoli and Deconstructed Pesto (page 41)

Greek Pita "Taco" (page 112)

Green Goddess Salmon Salad (page 113)

Greens with Chicken, Apple, and Blue Cheese (page 110)

Kale, Apple, and Brussels Sprout Salad (page 107)

Lemony Tilapia with Butter Lettuce and Herbs (page 122)

Lentil and Eggplant Stew with Apricots (page 38)

Lettuce Wraps with Tofu and Vegetables (page 87)

Lick-the-Bowl-Good Mushroom Soup (page 97)

Marinated Flank Steak with Thai Slaw (page 83)

Mediterranean Tuna Salad (page 102)

Pasta with Eggplant and Tomato Sauce (page 50)

Peanut Noodles with Snow Peas and Broccoli (page 36)

Pearl Couscous "Tabbouleh" (page 126)

Penne with Broccoli Rabe and White Beans (page 80)

Portobello and Poblano Tacos (page 42)

Rice Noodles with Shrimp, Bok Choy, and Mint (page 49)

Roasted Butternut Squash and Barley Stew (page 44)

Salmon Bowl with Asian Dipping Sauce (page 60)

Spinach and Mushroom Risotto (page 76)

Spinach Salad with Squash and Goat Cheese (page 106)

Stuffed Roasted Vegetable Sandwich (page 101)

Sweet Chili Fish Burgers with Cilantro Slaw (page 89)

Tortellini with Red Pepper Sauce (page 74)

White Bean, Jalapeño, and Kale Soup (page 104)

PANTRY MAGIC—LOOK WHAT'S
IN YOUR CUPBOARD

Barbecue Chicken Sandwiches (page 103)

Chickpea Burgers with Red Pepper Mayo (page 92)

Chunky Pasta and Bean Soup (page 114)

Lentil and Eggplant Stew with Apricots (page 38)

Lentil Salad with Tahini Dressing (page 117)

Mediterranean Tuna Salad (page 102)

Pan-Bagnat "Lite" (page 124)

Pasta with Eggplant and Tomato Sauce (page 50)

Spaghetti with Spicy Tomato and Olive Sauce (page 90)

Stuffed Peppers with Turkey and Olives (page 39)

PACK AND GO FOR NIGHTS ON THE RUN

Arugula and Kale Salad (page 99)

Barbecue Chicken Sandwiches (page 103)

Chicken and Roasted Grape Tartines (page 116)

Chicken Sandwiches with Avocado Salsa (page 118)

Chicken Waldorf Salad (page 125)

Chickpea Burgers with Red Pepper Mayo (page 92)

Cornmeal-Crusted Fish "Fry" with Caper Sauce (page 78)

Eggplant Parmesan Light (page 73)

Farro Salad with Feta and Fresh Herbs (page 98)

Greek Pita "Taco" (page 112)

Green Goddess Salmon Salad (page 113)

Greens with Chicken, Apple, and Blue Cheese (page 110)

Kale, Apple, and Brussels Sprout Salad (page 107)

Lentil Salad with Tahini Dressing (page 117)

Mediterranean Tuna Salad (page 102)

Pan-Bagnat "Lite" (page 124)

Pearl Couscous "Tabbouleh" (page 126)

Quinoa Salad with Cranberries and Mint (page 120)

Spinach Salad with Squash and Goat Cheese (page 106)

Stuffed Roasted Vegetable Sandwich (page 101)

Turkey-Mushroom Meatloaf (page 51)

JUST ADD A SALAD

Carrot and Parsnip Soup Two Ways (page 108)

Cauliflower and Leek Soup (page 128)

Chicken-Black Bean "Tamale" Casserole (page 43)

Chicken Soup with Meatballs and Greens (page 121)

Chunky Pasta and Bean Soup (page 114)

Double Creamy Grilled Cheese with Apple (page 96)

Easy One-Pot Chicken and Vegetables (page 91)

Eggplant Parmesan Light (page 73)

Four-Pepper Chicken Chili (page 59)

Fusilli with Broccoli and Deconstructed Pesto (page 41)

Lentil and Eggplant Stew with Apricots (page 38)

Lick-the-Bowl-Good Mushroom Soup (page 97)

Pasta with Eggplant and Tomato Sauce (page 50)

Penne with Broccoli Rabe and White Beans (page 80)

Roasted Butternut Squash and Barley Stew (page 44)

Seafood and Shellfish Stew (page 52)

Spaghetti with Spicy Tomato and Olive Sauce (page 90)

Spinach and Mushroom Risotto (page 76)

Stuffed Peppers with Turkey and Olives (page 39)

Stuffed Roasted Vegetable Sandwich (page 101)

Tortellini with Red Pepper Sauce (page 74)

White Bean, Jalapeño, and Kale Soup (page 104)

JUST ADD BREAD

Chicken Waldorf Salad (page 125)

Curried Vegetables (page 82)

Green Goddess Salmon Salad (page 113)

Greens with Chicken, Apple, and Blue Cheese (page 110)

Lemony Tilapia with Butter Lettuce and Herbs (page 122)

Mediterranean Tuna Salad (page 102)

Spinach Salad with Squash and Goat Cheese (page 106)

METRIC CONVERSIONS

WEIGHT

¼ ounce	7 grams
½ ounce	14 grams
1 ounce	28 grams
1 ½ ounces	42.5 grams
2 ounces	57 grams
3 ounces	85 grams
4 ounces	113 grams
6 ounces	170 grams
8 ounces	227 grams
16 ounces (1 pound)	454 grams

VOLUME

¼ teaspoon	1 ml
½ teaspoon	2.5 ml
¾ teaspoon	4 ml
1 teaspoon	5 ml
1 tablespoon	15 ml
¼ cup	59 ml
⅓ cup	79 ml
½ cup	118 ml
¾ cup	178 ml
1 cup	237 ml
2 cups (1 pint)	473 ml

INDEX

ADDITIONAL PHOTOGRAPHY CREDITS